Legal Pluralism

This book examines the development and fundamental nature of legal pluralism.

Legal pluralism evokes two distinctions: 'state' vs 'non-state' law; and 'law' vs 'non-law'. As such, although this book focuses upon circumstances in which two or more legal orders compete to govern the same social space, it also addresses the nature of law in general. Drawing on material conflicts arising within jurisdictions such as Australia, Burundi, Cameroon, Gambia, the United States, and Zambia, this book explores the conceptual, moral, and political challenges that legal pluralism creates. Emphasising that non-state law carries no less dignity than that often ascribed to the legal orders of contemporary states, it advances a theoretically sophisticated argument in favour of recognising and respecting genuine cases of legal pluralism, wherever they arise.

Accessible and thought provoking, this book will appeal to legal scholars, anthropologists, sociologists, and political and social philosophers as well as practising lawyers, judges, and policymakers who deal with issues of legal pluralism.

Alex Green is a Senior Lecturer at York Law School, University of York, and an Academic Associate of 23 Essex Street Chambers (London and Manchester), UK.

Jennifer Hendry is a Professor of Law and Social Justice at the University of Leeds School of Law and an Academic Associate of 23 Essex Street Chambers (London and Manchester), UK.

Part of the NEW TRAJECTORIES IN LAW Series

series editors
Adam Gearey, Birkbeck College, University of London
Prabha Kotiswaran, Kings College London
Colin Perrin, Commissioning Editor, Routledge
Mariana Valverde, University of Toronto

For information about the series and details of previous and forthcoming titles, see
www.routledge.com/New-Trajectories-in-Law/book-series/NTL

A GlassHouse Book

Legal Pluralism

New Trajectories in Law

Alex Green and Jennifer Hendry

Taylor & Francis Group
a GlassHouse Book

First published 2025
by Routledge
4 Park Square, Milton Park, Abingdon, Oxon
OX14 4RN

and by Routledge
605 Third Avenue, New York, NY 10158

Routledge is an imprint of the Taylor & Francis Group, an informa business

A GlassHouse book

© 2025 Alex Green and Jennifer Hendry

The right of Alex Green and Jennifer Hendry to be identified
as authors of this work has been asserted in accordance with
sections 77 and 78 of the Copyright, Designs and Patents Act 1988.

All rights reserved. No part of this book may be reprinted or
reproduced or utilised in any form or by any electronic, mechanical,
or other means, now known or hereafter invented, including
photocopying and recording, or in any information storage or
retrieval system, without permission in writing from the publishers.

Trademark notice: Product or corporate names may be
trademarks or registered trademarks, and are used only for
identification and explanation without intent to infringe.

British Library Cataloguing-in-Publication Data
A catalogue record for this book is available from the British Library

Library of Congress Cataloging-in-Publication Data
Names: Green, Alex, 1988– author. | Hendry, Jennifer, author.
Title: Legal pluralism : new trajectories in law / Alex Green
    and Jennifer Hendry.
Description: Abingdon, Oxon [UK] ; New York, NY :
    Routledge, 2024.
Series: New trajectories in law | Includes bibliographical
    references and index.
Identifiers: LCCN 2024027173 (print) | LCCN 2024027174
    (ebook) | ISBN 9780367487133 (hardback) | ISBN
    9781032873473 (paperback) | ISBN 9781003532149 (ebook)
Subjects: LCSH: Legal polycentricity.
Classification: LCC K236 .G74 2024 (print) | LCC K236
    (ebook) | DDC 340.9—dc23/eng/20240620
LC record available at https://lccn.loc.gov/2024027173
LC ebook record available at https://lccn.loc.gov/2024027174

ISBN: 978-0-367-48713-3 (hbk)
ISBN: 978-1-032-87347-3 (pbk)
ISBN: 978-1-003-53214-9 (ebk)

DOI: 10.4324/9781003532149

Typeset in Sabon
by Apex CoVantage, LLC

To our parents

Contents

Acknowledgements		*viii*
Introduction: A New Trajectory for Legal Pluralism		1
1	The Conceptual Development of Legal Pluralism	11
2	The Value(s) of Law and the Possibility of Its Plurality	35
3	Colonial Injustice and Legal Pluralism	60
	Conclusion: The Universal Plurality of Law	98
	Index	*104*

Acknowledgements

The argument and analysis that now comprise this book started life as a friendly, if initially somewhat entrenched, disagreement between fiancés. One of us, having been raised within the Dworkinian non-positivist tradition of analytical legal philosophy, was utterly convinced that law must be understood as a single domain of normative value, such that any talk of its plurality or 'messiness' must rest on some kind of fundamental mistake. Thankfully, the other one of us knew better, and their good sense prevailed. What survived from this disagreement, however, was a shared sense that maybe, at some level, both of us were right in ways that really mattered. With that thought in mind, we set about writing a paper together one rainy afternoon on the 47th floor of a Hong Kong apartment building. Thanks are due to Michael Palmer for his early support of that smaller project, which would not have gone anywhere near as smoothly without him.

Sometime later, at an annual conference of the United Kingdom Socio-Legal Studies Association, Colin Perrin at Routledge Glasshouse suggested that an extended version of our argument might make for an interesting addition to their *New Trajectories in Law* series. Thanks are due to him for this suggestion and for his continued support, encouragement, and patience throughout the writing process. As our argument developed, very many people were generous with their comments and criticisms. It is impossible to list them all by name, but particular thanks are due to the following people. Margaret Davies, David Dyzenhaus, Alexandra Hearne, Joshua Jowitt, Simon Palmer, Harrison Singh, Dimitrios Tsarapatsanis, and Scott Veitch each provided a wealth of feedback on the philosophical elements of our argument that challenged and enriched our understanding of both legal pluralism and law in general. On the more contextual elements of our position, particular thanks are due to N. Bruce Duthu and Melissa Tatum, who provided invaluable guidance on the concrete injustices and inequities facing many Indigenous peoples today. Without their support, this text would lack much of the nuance we hope that it has come to possess. In broader academic terms, thanks are also due to TT Arvind, Simon Halliday, Elies van Sliedregt, and Simon NM Young for their support, as well as to the wonderful academic communities of Juris North, the Socio-Legal Studies Association, the UCL Legal Philosophy Forum, and both the audience and presenters at the University of Leeds *Cosmopolitan Pluralism and International Criminal Justice Conference.*

Writing even a short-form monograph such as this can be a stressful and tiring experience, so we would also like to give thanks to Naomi Round Cahalin and the other members of the production team at Routledge for their efforts and forbearance. Final and particular thanks are also due to Gillian and Timothy Green and to James and Jean Hendry for their love and encouragement. It may seem trite for academics to ascribe their own love and respect for learning to the influence of their parents, but for both of us, this is a profound truth. This book simply would never have been written had they not raised us in the way that they did. We both owe them all such a very great deal.

Introduction

A New Trajectory for Legal Pluralism

1. Introduction

This book is about legal pluralism: what it is and why it matters. We treat these two questions as necessarily linked, such that our answer to the first question turns substantially upon our views in relation to the second. Indeed, part of our purpose in this book is to establish an approach to the moral and political importance of legal pluralism that is distinct from but nonetheless continuous with many of those that have come before. Throughout our argument, we address a number of connected questions, including the nature of law, the requirements of the Rule of Law, the demands of political legitimacy, and the value of collective self-determination. Our overall approach, to the extent that such things need labelling, is best classified as 'socio-legal jurisprudence'. Our arguments about the nature of law and legal pluralism fall squarely within the philosophy of law. However, our construction of these positions is led by attention to the concrete social contexts within which law is experienced and practised by those to whom it applies rather than solely with reference to *a priori* principles or by reflection upon our own intuitions. Moreover, although the position we adopt within the second half of this text can be more or less accurately described as 'non-positivist' or else as falling within the 'natural law' tradition,[1] we place deliberate emphasis upon the diverse range of law-related beliefs and experiences that historically embedded legal subjects possess.[2] Our aim is to

---

1 For non-positivism in general, see: Liam Murphy, *What Makes Law: An Introduction to The Philosophy of Law* (CUP 2014) ch 4; Mark Greenberg, 'The Moral Impact Theory of Law' (2014) 123(5) Yale LJ 1288.

2 Hitherto, both natural law and non-positivism more broadly have come up rather short in this respect, insofar as they draw neigh-completely upon the (almost wholly Western and characteristically male) moral and ethical intuitions of their authors, together with citations to other scholars who tend towards the same. For a particularly egregious

DOI: 10.4324/9781003532149-1

2 Introduction

develop a deliberately inclusive conception of law which nonetheless makes intelligible the idea that the diverse and often conflicting legal orders currently in existence form a significant part of our moral and political world.

In addition to advancing this discrete perspective, we aim also to recognise and celebrate the 'plurality of pluralities' that exists within the extensive scholarly literature on legal pluralism that has developed over the last several decades (see Chapter 1). Legal pluralism, as we seek to demonstrate in what follows, is no less a contested concept than law itself; it may even be 'essentially contested'.[3] Indeed, it is perhaps because the concept of law admits so many contrary interpretations that the possibility of 'plural legality' offers such a unique opportunity for anthropological, sociological, and philosophical reflection. The first chapter of this text is dedicated in large part to canvassing these diverse perspectives and so can be read largely in isolation from the final two chapters, within which our positive argument is developed. At various points, we note the ways in which our positive arguments are inspired by large swaths of this earlier writing. In particular, our focus on postcolonial and settler-state contexts as paradigmatic of legal pluralism draws substantially upon the anthropological heritage of early scholarship on that topic, while the normative importance we place upon governmental legitimacy and collective self-determination as requirements of social justice is contiguous with the moral and political positions adopted by many scholars writing on legal pluralism within the critical tradition.

Due to these twin ambitions, this book functions partly as an argumentative monograph and partly as an introductory text. It is not, however, a textbook, and we cannot hope to be truly exhaustive in relation to the full range of relevant scholarship that a longer and more sustained summary of this field might admit. We hope nonetheless to furnish those new to the study of legal pluralism with solid ground upon which to stand as they pursue its conceptual trajectory from historical development to contemporary debates. Moreover, for those who are already familiar with the complexities created by the phenomenon of plural legal orders functioning within the same social space, we hope to offer a fresh perspective on why these (often controversial) situations are worthy of academic attention. In what remains of this introduction, with

---

recent example, see: Adrian Vermeule, *Common Good Constitutionalism: Recovering the Classical Legal Tradition* (Polity 2022) chs 1 and 5.

3 WB Gallie, 'Essentially Contested Concepts' (1955–56) 56 Proceedings of the Aristotelian Society 167.

these aims and hopes in mind, we briefly establish the structure of the book before making some observations about the challenges that can be experienced when teaching and learning about legal pluralism within contemporary Western settings.

2. Structure of the Text

The text that follows is divided into three substantive chapters followed by a short conclusion. Chapter 1 provides a road map for those new to the concept of legal pluralism. Beginning with the idea of legally pluralist thinking as an empirical and theoretical response to state-centric views of law, it delivers a step-by-step account of the main considerations and debates at each stage of that concept's development. Departing from the anthropological roots of legal pluralism and the well-known distinction between 'weak' and 'strong' versions of that concept, we then address what we call 'The Law Question': whether or not 'non-state law' can properly be included within a philosophically rigorous understanding of law in general. Next, we problematise descriptive accounts of law generally, starting with a critique of legal positivism alongside discussion of 'social fact legal pluralism' and concluding with the eventual turn by some philosophers towards the label 'normative pluralism'. Our discussion then progresses to 'interlegality', a theoretical perspective quite different from the aesthetic of ordered coherence found within more orthodox jurisprudence, and then to a critique of Western ethnocentric legal thought alongside conceptually connected imperial practices of colonisation and dispossession. Chapter 1 then concludes by introducing 'critical legal pluralism' and flagging the connection between this moral and political project and our own non-positivist approach.

Chapter 2 establishes the theoretical framework for our own account of legal pluralism, which adopts a discretely non-positivist methodology.[4] According to this approach, the existence of law in any given social space is contingent upon particular facts about political morality, which we understand to concern the genuine normative reasons that relate to how human communities should conduct themselves at a collective level.[5] In particular, what interests us is whether or not

---

4 For an early characterisation of our approach, see: Alex Green and Jennifer Hendry, 'Non-Positivist Legal Pluralism and Crises of Legitimacy in Settler States' (2019) 14(2) Journal of Comparative Law 267.

5 On genuine normative reasons, see: Derek Parfit, *On What Matters*, vol 1 (OUP 2011) 31. On political morality, see: Ronald Dworkin, *Justice for Hedgehogs* (Harvard UP 2011) 327–50.

4 Introduction

a given set of governance traditions being practised within a particular space instantiate the values of 'legality' or, as it is often called, the Rule of Law. Our analysis begins with an account of why it is sensible and important to interrogate the existence of both law and legal pluralism in this normatively engaged manner. We then turn to the idea of legality itself, describing what it requires in concrete terms and what other political values it depends upon to flesh out its prescriptive content. This is crucial to our overall approach because it is the presence or absence of legality as a set of political values that determines for us whether a given set of governance practices should be considered law. Having advanced this general theoretical position, we then introduce a philosophical puzzle we call the 'problem of plural legality'. This proceeds as follows: our understanding of legality emphasises the normative importance of individuals being governed in relation to a single set of norms, which seems to indicate that the very idea of legal pluralism conflicts with the values upon which we say the existence of law turns. How can law be both unifying and plural? We suggest that, in particular social contexts, legality itself both explains and justifies this apparent paradox. The very same values that ordinarily mandate societies to organise themselves with reference to a single set of governing norms can, on occasion, mandate that a plurality of governing orders should be maintained instead. In such circumstances, most attempts to 'dissolve' legal pluralism by promoting the dominance of one order over another would not only be unjust but would also run contrary to the normative foundations of legality itself. After making these claims, we then establish another important normative dimension to our overall approach: that wherever an independent legal order is established, a discrete means for collective self-determination also arises. This provides a weighty reason for both law and legal pluralism to be recognised and respected.

Chapter 3 turns from the establishment of our general approach to the application of that theory. Our focus throughout is legal pluralism within postcolonial and settler-states, which we take to be both paradigmatic and most clearly illustrative of legal pluralism in general. Drawing upon disputes within the administration of criminal justice, those concerning the use and reverence due to sacred sites, and others surrounding the regulation of land, we contend that apparent conflicts between two or more putative legal orders can be used to confirm the existence of legal pluralism within a range of settings affected by the injustice of colonialism. Moreover, approaching the same analytical task at a more abstract and global scale, we argue for the complicity of contemporary international law in creating the very circumstances of injustice that both prompt and threaten the fragile and indispensable existence of legal pluralism within colonial and postcolonial settings. Our analysis in

Introduction   5

this chapter begins with a general characterisation of why our conception of legal pluralism is apt to arise within states that possess colonial legacies. Our focus is upon the legacies of historical injustice created by colonialism and the implications of these legacies for the instantiation of legality (and its constitutive values) within such states. At bottom, our claim is that postcolonial and settler-states frequently experience legal pluralism because the normative profiles of these states are tainted by their colonial pasts, as well as the related and contemporary injustices that persist within them. The effect of this is to make it much harder for state law to assert itself against non-state law within those social spaces in any kind of justifiable manner. Within circumstances like these, legal pluralism can be confirmed through philosophical reflection combined with attention to socio-legal reality.

Deliberately absent from both the intellectual history outlined in Chapter 1, as well as from the non-positivist account of legal pluralism within Chapters 2 and 3, is reflection upon either 'global legal pluralism' or 'constitutional pluralism', both of which have generated a significant body of additional literature.[6] Insofar as they utilise the idea of plural and interacting normative orders, which was originally developed for examining the modes of legal pluralism this book does discuss,[7] both global legal pluralism and constitutional pluralism are extensions of that core idea into new intellectual terrain rather than revisions or reinterpretations of the idea itself. In a nutshell, global legal pluralism addresses the (actual and perceived) conflicts of practical authority that arise from the interaction between multiple legal and 'quasi-legal' orders that exist within, beyond, and between states.[8] Constitutional pluralism, by contrast, concerns the 'post-Westphalian' fragmentation of constitutional authority, institutions, and principles both within and away from the state towards

---

6 For example, on the former, see: Paul Berman (ed), *The Oxford Handbook of Global Legal Pluralism* (OUP 2020); Michael Helfand (ed), *Negotiating State and Non-State Law: The Challenges of Global and Local Legal Pluralism* (CUP 2015); Elies van Sliedregt and Paul Berman (eds), *International Criminal Law and Legal Pluralism: Straddling Cosmopolitan Aims and Distribution Enforcement* (OUP 2020); Anna Jurkevics, 'Democracy in Contested Territory: On the Legitimacy of Global Legal Pluralism' (2022) 25(2) Critical Review of International Social and Political Philosophy 187; Sally Merry, 'Global Legal Pluralism and the Temporality of Soft Law' (2014) 46(1) Journal of Legal Pluralism and Unofficial Law 108. On the latter, again for example, see: Klemen Jaklic, *Constitutional Pluralism in the EU* (OUP 2014); Matej Avbelj and Jan Komárek (ed), *Constitutional Pluralism in the European Union and Beyond* (Hart 2012); Jean Cohen, *Globalisation and Sovereignty: Rethinking Legality, Legitimacy, and Constitutionalism* (CUP 2012); Gavin Anderson, *Constitutional Rights after Globalization* (Hart 2005); Cormac MacAmhlaigh, *New Constitutional Horizons: Towards a Pluralist Constitutional Theory* (OUP 2022).
7 On state-internal constellations of legal pluralism, see chapter 1.
8 Paul Berman, *Global Legal Pluralism* (CUP 2012) 23–58, 141–51.

6 Introduction

substate, international, and transnational practices and organisations.[9] The application of our own theory to these questions, particularly given their international context and implications, would require a text of far greater length than the one presented here. Our primary concern is with what we take to be the conceptual core of legal pluralism itself: the phenomenon of two or more normative orders, both claiming the essence and plenary authority of law, making independently plausible but nonetheless inconsistent claims to govern the same social space. Whether or how that core idea might illuminate inter- and trans-state conflicts in practical or political authority we leave, for now at least, to others.

3. Teaching and Learning about Legal Pluralism

In our joint experience, the challenges posed by legal pluralism in classroom settings fall into two broad categories. First, there are those that arise from the multidisciplinary nature of the literature that established and interrogates the concept. Second, there are those arising from the incredible cultural, political, and social diversity of the communities within which legal pluralism can arise. Taking the first, students and teachers both may find intimidating the shear breadth and diversity of legally pluralist thought. Works of anthropology, sociology, critical theory, analytical philosophy, and comparative law all shed light on the phenomenon of legal pluralism (for an indication of this, see Chapter 1). Although many legal scholars would now consider themselves either inter- or even multidisciplinary to some degree, parsing this material accurately, not to mention structing it into or within a sufficiently accessible undergraduate or taught postgraduate syllabus, can be a daunting task. For instance, students within modules on comparative law or legal theory might not expect to be provided within anthropological or sociological material and, in any event, may have no prior experience of reading and discussing such work. Teachers will need to be aware of this and adjust their expectations accordingly. In our experience, when such multidisciplinary engagement goes well, students tend to find the diversity of material to which they are exposed refreshing and even inspiring, particularly when contrasted with their more exclusively doctrinal and non-comparative studies.

There is another side to this, however. Notwithstanding the multidisciplinary nature of legally pluralist literature, students and teachers

---

9 Neil Walker, 'The Idea of Constitutional Pluralism' (2002) 55(3) MLR 317.

Introduction 7

may also discover an unwillingness on the part of at least some authors to acknowledge the value of engaging across disciplines in the requisite manner. For instance, within analytical legal philosophy, there is a relatively commonplace perception that the study of the nature of law (or 'general jurisprudence' as it is often called)[10] must not only remain neutral across jurisdictions but also when it comes to geographical space or historical period.[11] On this basis, it is not unusual for those who hold this view to neglect anthropological and sociological reflection on the nature of law in its entirety. More fundamentally, some scholars write as though general jurisprudence itself were exhausted by Western, Anglo-American analytical traditions of legal philosophy, such that any writing outwith those traditions falls out of scope for taxonomical reasons.[12] Even more austerely, some claim it to be exhausted by a particular mode of enquiry within that tradition, such as what is often referred to as 'conceptual analysis'.[13] Such academic bunker-building can be frustrating for teachers and alienating for students, particularly those who come from non-Western backgrounds.

Against this somewhat disheartening trend, we can urge little more than an attitude of optimism and patience. Within our own teaching, we have found that exposing students to diverse conceptions of law dramatically improves their ability to reason creatively within comparative and theoretical modules.[14] To pick just one such anecdote, Aboriginal Australian legal scholar Irene Watson's account 'from the inside, about [her] law and life ways which are buried alive by a dominant colonising culture' has been of considerable use to us both when introducing students to traditions of legal knowledge starkly different from their own.[15] In pedagogical terms, Watson's quotation of a story 'known throughout Aboriginal Australia' is characteristically highly successful when it comes to engaging both our students'

---

10 Leslie Green, 'General Jurisprudence: A 25th Anniversary Essay' (2005) 25 OJLS 565; Tarunabh Khaitan and Sandy Steel, 'Areas of Law: Three Questions in Special Jurisprudence' (2023) 43(1) OJLS 76.

11 Green (n 10) 565–67; Joseph Raz, *The Authority of Law: Essays on Law and Morality* (Clarendon Press 1979) 104–5.

12 Martin Krygier, 'The Concept of Law and Social Theory' (1982) 2 OJLS 155, 157. This need not be so, see: Julie Dickson, *Elucidating Law* (OUP 2022) 25–53.

13 We infer this from the tone and general content of, for example: Jules Coleman, *The Practice of Principle: In Defence of a Pragmatist Approach to Legal Theory* (OUP 2003) 175–218.

14 See further: Alex Green, 'Lines to a Don: Why It is Isn't Mindless to "Reimagine" Jurisprudence' (2023) 57(4) The Law Teacher 548.

15 Irene Watson, 'Buried Alive' (2002) 13(1) Law and Critique 253.

8 Introduction

imagination and their critical reasoning skills.[16] This is worth reproducing in full:

> In the beginning there lived a giant frog, who drank up all the water until there was no water left in the creeks lagoons rivers lakes and even the oceans. All the animals became thirsty and came together to find a solution that would satisfy their growing thirst. The animals decided the way to do this was to get the frog to release the water back to the land, and that the 'proper' way to do this was to make the frog laugh. After much performing one of the animals found a way to humour the frog, until it released a great peal of laughter. When the frog laughed it released all the water, it came gushing back to the land filling creeks, riverbeds, lakes and even the oceans. As the community of animals once again turned their gaze to the frog they realised they had to make the large frog transform into a smaller one, so that it could no longer dominate the community. They decided to reduce the one large frog to many much smaller frogs, so that the frog would be brought to share equally with all other living beings.

This parable can be usefully compared to Western philosophical myths about the creation of law and the adoption of new legal orders, such as the 'state of nature' and the 'social contract' (found, for example, in the work of Thomas Hobbes).[17] Engaging with such diverse ways of writing about law can present students with a steep learning curve, particularly at undergraduate level, and care must be taken not to overwhelm them with the full diversity of methods and traditions available. This is an easy mistake to make, particularly given the independently important process of decolonising our legal curriculums and the need for substantive inclusivity that process characteristically entails.[18] Nonetheless, in our view at least, the benefits of pushing out this particular boat far outweigh the costs.

Turning to the second set of potential challenges, students will almost certainly need careful introduction to the extraordinary diversity of non-state law. If this is not managed carefully, students may mistakenly assume that 'non-state law', which is best viewed as categorisation by exclusion to the extent that it has any overarching meaning at all, denotes normative orders with some shared set of essential features beyond their legality itself. This could be scarcely further from the truth and teachers

---

16 ibid.
17 Thomas Hobbes, *Leviathan or The Matter, Forme and Power of a Commonwealth Ecclesiasticall and Civil* (JCA Gaskin ed, OUP 1996) chs XIII–XVIII.
18 Folúkẹ́ Adébísí, *Decolonisation and Legal Knowledge* (Bristol UP 2023) Conclusion.

should take great pains to avoid such conflation. Elision between the many and varied Indigenous legal orders that exist within settler and postcolonial states is particularly hazardous, since it tempts essentialising and racist suggestions that Indigenous peoples the world over somehow comprise a unified set with characteristics defined primarily in terms of their indigeneity rather than by their particular cultures, histories, and practices.[19] Similar hazards are to be found in treating all religious legal orders as somehow equivalent or by running them together with tribal or familial legal orders with significant spiritual elements, which, for example, might not share many essential features of religious law in Abrahamic contexts. Our point here is not that useful generalisations about particular groups of non-state legal orders are altogether impossible, only that sweeping taxonomies are more likely to mislead students than to inform them.

A subsequent and connected challenge is that given the importance of examining different legal orders within their proper cultural, political, and social contexts, students and teachers both may feel that understanding anything about legal pluralism at all requires them to have already gained considerable freestanding knowledge of each and every tradition of law implicated within a particular instance of normative plurality. This is an understandable concern, albeit one that risks overstating the demands of good scholarship and careful instruction. As we note in Chapter 2, an attitude of relative humility goes a long way when thinking about traditions within which one is not culturally embedded, and the intensity at which this attitude is consciously maintained both can and should be adjusted upwards when approaching situations marked by colonial domination and other imbalances of power. For the purposes of classroom teaching and module assessment, it will often be sufficient to acknowledge explicitly whatever limitations in knowledge and understanding an individual may have, with the proviso that such admissions neither can nor should wholly replace good-faith attempts at cross-cultural understanding, appropriately augmented by careful study and critical reflection.

The study of legal pluralism is challenging precisely because it amounts to no more or less than an attempt to understand the nature and condition of law as it exists within the real world, beset as that is by the messy and complicating historical contingencies so often excluded from philosophical thought experiments. Our aim in this text is to provide a framing that lays some of these contingencies bare, says something cogent and informative about them, and provokes our readers into asking why they matter. As the intellectual history contained within Chapter 1 makes clear, the

---

19 For the history and dangers of such essentialisation, see: Linda Tuhiwai Smith, *Decolonizing Methodologies: Research and Indigenous Peoples* (3rd edn, Bloomsbury 2021) chs 2–4.

10   Introduction

non-positivist approach we outline in Chapters 2 and 3 is just one way of accomplishing this. Insofar as it focuses on connections between the existence of law and the possibility of social justice, our approach is instrumentally useful. Insofar as it implies a general methodological position within legal philosophy, it may even be conceptually or metaphysically 'correct'. But that alone does not matter. We hope above all for it to be *clear*, such that this book will aid you in reasoning carefully and systematically about the 'recalcitrant social reality' that legal pluralism represents.[20]

---

20   John Griffiths, 'What is Legal Pluralism?' (1986) 24 Journal of Legal Pluralism and Unofficial Law 1.

Chapter 1

The Conceptual Development of Legal Pluralism

1. Introduction

In this chapter, our aim is to provide an overview of the intellectual origins and development of legally pluralist thinking, to highlight significant stages and points of departure, and to explain the disciplinary, conceptual, and methodological divergences that arise as a result. We intend this chapter to be a guide for readers through the interdisciplinary history of legal pluralism: identifying the major voices in the relevant debates, stressing important overlaps and disconnections across different conceptualisations, and providing a clear introduction to the terminology and concepts associated with legally pluralist approaches. In terms of the positive argument we develop in Chapters 2 and 3, this exercise in intellectual history provides essential background for the novel claims we make hereafter.

Taking a broadly chronological approach, we chart the beginnings of legal pluralism as a key concept in social and cultural anthropology and the study of colonial and postcolonial societies before shifting our focus to the wide-ranging debates concerning legality, normativity, rules, institutions, and the fault lines between state and non-state practices. In doing so, we follow an established trend within the literature by differentiating between two broad understandings of legal pluralism: *empirical* and *theoretical*. Palmer and Zhou elaborate on these umbrella approaches, distinguishing them as, on the one hand, 'legal pluralism empirically located in specific social, cultural and historical contexts, and a more theoretically inclined legal pluralism constructed by analysts searching for a better understanding of the nature of law and, by extension, the role of law in legal systems'[1] on the other. By cleaving to Palmer and Zhou's distinction, we hope to present the relevant interdisciplinary literature in a manner that is both faithful to its historical development

---

1 Michael Palmer and Ling Zhou, 'Legal Pluralism' in Jan M Smits and others (eds), *Elgar Encyclopaedia of Comparative Law* (Edward Elgar 2023) part IV, 3–4.

DOI: 10.4324/9781003532149-2

12 The Conceptual Development of Legal Pluralism

and accessible for unfamiliar readers. Our own account of legal pluralism, developed in subsequent chapters, fits somewhat awkwardly across this split: although it is explicitly theoretical in nature (see Chapter 2), it draws substantially upon empirical particularity (Chapter 3).

A small caveat before proceeding. Since its emergence in the 1960s, the phrase 'legal pluralism' has been used in a variety of contexts to denote different things, with the result that its points of reference have become somewhat stretched. Our goal here is not to try to reconcile these different conceptions. Indeed, the innovative 'non-positivist' conception of legal pluralism articulated in Chapters 2 and 3 possesses both similarities and points of divergence to many of the different views we detail here. Our aim is rather to highlight how and why these views came about, where their respective points of emphasis lie, and where they sit relative to others in these ongoing discussions.

This chapter has the following structure. First, it engages with the idea of legally pluralist thinking as an empirical and theoretical response to state-centric views of law, and it delivers a step-by-step account of the main considerations and debates at each stage of that concept's development. Beginning with its anthropological heritage and the well-known distinction between 'weak' and 'strong' legal pluralism (Section 2), our discussion then covers the interdisciplinary engagement with what we call 'The Law Question', that is, whether or not 'non-state law' can properly be included within a philosophically rigorous understanding of law in general (Section 3). Noting the arrival of the analytical legal philosophers at the party, next, we problematise descriptive accounts of law generally: this starts with a critical account of legal positivism alongside discussion of 'social fact legal pluralism' and concludes with the eventual turn by some philosophers towards the label 'normative pluralism' (Section 4). Following this conceptual trajectory into legal multiplicity, our discussion progresses to 'interlegality', a theoretical perspective far removed from the aesthetic of ordered coherence found within more traditional, modern(ist) jurisprudence (Section 5), and then to a critical discussion of Western ethnocentric legal thought alongside its practical corollary: imperial practices of colonisation and dispossession (Section 6). Chapter 1 then concludes by introducing critical legal pluralist ideas and flagging the connection between their moral and political project and our own non-positivist legal pluralist approach (Section 7).

2. Legal Pluralism and 'The Messy Compromise'

When embarking on a discussion of legal pluralism, it is useful to juxtapose the very idea of plural legalities – that is, different legal orders existing within the same social space – with one of its most important conceptual opposites, what John Griffiths named the 'ideology of legal centralism'. This is the view that:

> [L]aw is and should be the law of the state, uniform for all persons, exclusive of all other law, and administered by a single set of state institutions. To the extent that other, lesser normative orderings, such as the church, the family, the voluntary association and the economic organization exist, they ought to be and in fact are hierarchically subordinate to the law and institutions of the state.[2]

Legally pluralist thinking can thus be seen as a challenge to the basic legal centralist idea that *only state law* may be properly characterised *as law*. Indeed, Griffiths refers to legal centralism as an ideology because of the manner in which a vital link is forged between the state – 'the fundamental unit of political organization' – and the idea of law as 'a single, unified and exclusive hierarchical normative ordering'.[3] This state-centralist conception is indicative of fundamentally Westphalian thinking, whereby 'two entangled strands of politico-legal development gained momentum, the nation state and its political counterpart, the imperial and colonial state [. . . and] entailed the axiomatic shift from "where there is society, there is law" to "where there is state, there is law"'.[4] Such state-oriented centralism is also, in one important sense, legally *monist* insofar as it considers legal orders to exist if and only if statehood is also present: the notion that there might be other, non-state social sources of law is wholly alien to that conception.[5]

Scholars taking a legally pluralist view take issue with this identification of statehood with legality, arguing not only that it is factually incorrect in many societies but also that it gives rise to a problematically essentialist and sloppily ahistorical understanding of law. This then tempts the question: why and how did this idea of state law become so powerful that it not only became the presumptive understanding of legal ordering but also generated and maintained a counterfactual hegemony? Why is this mis-description, this illusion, so seductive? For Griffiths, there are two reasons for this. First, the ascendance of centralism can be explained in relation to how 'conceptions of what law *is* have reflected a particular idea about what it *ought* to be'[6] and, second, the beguiling notion that the law ought to be ordered, tidy, organised,

---

2 John Griffiths, 'What is Legal Pluralism?' (1986) 18(24) Journal of Legal Pluralism and Unofficial Law 1–55, 3.

3 ibid.

4 Keebet von Benda-Beckmann and Bertram Turner, 'Legal Pluralism, Social Theory, and the State' (2018) 50(3) Journal of Legal Pluralism and Unofficial Law 255, 256.

5 For more on legal monism as such, see the Conclusion to this book.

6 Griffiths (n 2) 4, emphasis added.

14 The Conceptual Development of Legal Pluralism

consistent, and coherent. This 'modern' legal aesthetic inclination towards coherence is something Margaret Davies highlights, noting that '[p]hilosophers and theorists have often tended to prefer conceptual order and clarity over disorder and ambiguity'.[7] She further explains that '[n]otions such as pedigree, purity, integrity, closure, hierarchy, and unity represent the unargued preferences of theorists who have removed or simplified human beings with their messy experiences and interpretations'.[8] This predilection becomes apparent when we look more closely at what ideas underpin descriptions of law as 'an exclusive, systematic and unified hierarchical ordering of normative propositions'.[9] As Griffiths notes, the uniting aspect comes either top-down, from a sovereign or otherwise apex directive, or bottom-up, as in the case of Kelsen's *Grundnorm* or Hart's rule of recognition.[10] These theoretical standpoints are buttressed, explains Griffiths, by the 'factual power of the state', namely the 'keystone of an otherwise normative system, which affords the empirical condition for the actual existence of "law"'.[11] His criticism here is that this 'state plus law' combination has the unwelcome effect of presenting itself as the only show in town, as it were: as an idealised picture of law in modern societies, a picture that other normative orders must emulate or otherwise fail to meet the necessary threshold of 'law'.

The legal pluralist challenge to legal centralism can thus be understood as a challenge to this tidy deception, a rejection of this unrepresentative picture of legality, and a recognition that, while the image of law as 'conceptually limited and hierarchically structured, with a determinate centre and orderly spaces' is practically convenient,[12] it is and remains an illusion. As Franz von Benda-Beckmann put it, this debate revolves around the issue of 'whether or not one is prepared to admit the *theoretical possibility* of more than one legal order or mechanism within one socio-political space, based on different sources of ultimate validity and maintained by forms of organization other than the state'.[13] To be open to legal pluralism is to be open to the dynamic and contested *messiness* of legal reality. We share many of these concerns, as will be evident from our argument in Chapter 2. Although the account we develop there makes a set of universal claims about the value of law and its unifying function within the collective self-determination of peoples, we firmly

---

7 Margaret Davies, *Law Unlimited* (Routledge 2018) 4.
8 ibid 5.
9 Griffiths (n 2) 3.
10 ibid.
11 ibid.
12 Davies (n 7) 5.
13 Franz von Benda-Beckmann, 'Who's Afraid of Legal Pluralism?' (2002) 34(47) Journal of Legal Pluralism and Unofficial Law 37.

The Conceptual Development of Legal Pluralism 15

resist any suggestion that this value or function shares any necessary connection to the state or that it can be meaningfully divorced from the diverse modes of instantiation through which it appears, often messily and always imperfectly, within concrete social reality.

Considering the dominance of the state-centric, *monist* conception of law, however, it is not surprising that scholars engaged in the task of trying to describe and chart legal diversity started out by characterising normative orders in terms of what they were not, that is, *non-state* law. This state/non-state dichotomy informed much early thinking about legal pluralism and gave rise to some initial conceptual categorisations, notably Griffiths's 'weak' and Sally Engle Merry's 'classic' legal pluralism. Although not precisely identical, these are similar enough to be considered together.

Griffiths's weak form of legal pluralism, which tends to be associated with the existence of more than one legal order within the same *state*, and within postcolonial states in particular, has three main features. First, the official recognition of non-state law, which is indispensable when identifying cases of weak legal pluralism, is in the gift of the state. Second, the state benefits from this conciliation, insofar as its function as the recognising entity serves largely to cement its perceived plenary authority. Third, weak legal pluralism is usually seen as temporary, insofar as it is a workaround solution or managerial technique that hegemonic states use for dealing with complex circumstances: 'the messy compromise [that] the ideology of legal centralism feels itself obliged to make with recalcitrant social reality'.[14] As such, although this 'weak' form of legal pluralism supersedes the monist, centralist form, it remains (from one perspective at least) tepid and uninspiring, largely due to the fact that its underlying ideology remains, at bottom, centralist. This holds because of what the authority to bestow 'weak' legal pluralism says about state power: such pluralism exists only where a difference is recognised and managed by a hegemonic state legal order. State recognition is crucial and, moreover, is both ultimately determined and procedurally conditioned through recourse to the very same authoritative sources as all other state law. From a legally pluralist perspective, this is all fairly unsatisfying, and Griffiths is contemptuous in his dismissal of this weak form's claim to the description of legal pluralism proper, condemning it as derivative of a legally centralist hierarchy whereby the recognised law is inescapably seen as inferior to that of the recognising power. Davies cites Aboriginal and Torres Strait Islander land entitlement as managed by the Australian common and statutory law on native title as an example of this form, noting that:

in a weak sense, Australian law has recognised Indigenous law on this issue, but it is a recognition which does not subvert the basic

---

14 Griffiths (n 2) 7.

16 The Conceptual Development of Legal Pluralism

centralist dogma of Australian law, because it is fully effected within that law. Native title illustrates a continuation of standard colonial practices (in Australia and elsewhere), whereby Indigenous laws can achieve some status, but strictly within the framework of colonial recognition. The recognition of such differences as Federal/State and European law/Indigenous law, to the extent that they are contained within dominant law, are no threat to the doctrine of centralism because they are structurally subsumed within state law. With 'weak' pluralism there is no 'irreducible outness', because the law which might otherwise be regarded as 'out' is in fact controlled by the system.[15]

Much like this weak form, Merry's 'classic' or 'classical' conception of legal pluralism concerns the traditional anthropological and sociological analysis of 'the intersections of indigenous and European law' in colonised societies.[16] Indeed, the classic form specifically concerns (post)colonial societies, where interactions between the state legal order and Indigenous, customary, imperial, and/or imposed laws were generative of circumstances of plural legality. Merry even highlights how 'research on legal pluralism began in the study of colonial societies in which an imperialist nation, equipped with a centralized and codified legal system, imposed this system on societies with far different legal systems, often unwritten and lacking formal structures for judging and punishing'.[17] A leading legal anthropologist, Merry's opinion of classic legal pluralism differs from Griffiths's categorical dismissal of the weak form: although not insensible to how classic legal pluralism is 'embedded in relations of unequal power', she also notes its 'sophisticated theoretical traditions and rich ethnography' as well as outlining its significant contributions:

> First is the analysis of the interaction between normative orders that are fundamentally different in their underlying conceptual structure. Second is an attention to the elaboration of customary law as historically derived. Third is the delineation of the dialectic between normative orders. In classic legal pluralism, this dialectic takes place in situations in which different orders are readily identified and the dynamics of resistance and restructuring by groups experiencing the imposition of a very different normative order are relatively easy to see.[18]

It is worth noting here that, following legal anthropological and legal sociological traditions respectively, both Merry and Griffiths are

---

15 Margaret Davies, 'The Ethos of Pluralism' (2005) 27(1) Sydney LR 87, 93.
16 Sally Engle Merry, 'Legal Pluralism' (1988) 22(5) Law and Society Review 869, 872.
17 ibid 874.
18 ibid 873.

concerned primarily with empiricist-positivist identifications and descriptions of situations within which legal pluralism might be thought to arise. Specifically, they are concerned with discovering those sets of circumstances 'in which behaviour pursuant to more than one legal order occurs' and exploring those circumstances to illuminate their particular cultural, historical, and social contexts.[19] Their focus was thus largely on plurality and not legality, a distinction which comes much more obviously to the fore a little later on. While maintaining an empirical approach, the respective discussions of 'strong' and 'new' legal pluralism help to pave the way for this disciplinary and focal pivot towards questions about the nature or essence *of law*, as the next section explains.

3. Legal Pluralism and 'The Law Question'

Strong, deep, or new legal pluralism, broadly stated, can be understood as a means of severing what previously had been considered by many to be the necessary connection between law and the state. Unlike weak or classic legal pluralism, where the relationship between state law and *recognised* law is predetermined, strong or new legal pluralism acknowledges that there are myriad forms of ordering 'pertain[ing] to members of a society that are not necessarily dependent upon the state for recognition of their authority'.[20] This form of legal pluralism originates 'from the sociological understanding of law as independent of the state and empirically found as a coexistence of various legal orders, rather than as a single system',[21] and thus counteracts the inclination, discussed earlier, 'to think of all legal ordering as rooted in state law'.[22] Davies's definition of this strong form is worth quoting at length:

> 'strong' legal pluralism means essentially that the difference or otherness upon which the understanding of pluralism is based cannot be reduced to the singular authority of a state. There is 'strong' legal pluralism where two or more 'laws' exist in the one place and there is no dominant or overarching system which orders the relations between the different laws. To take once more the example of colonialism, the recognition of Indigenous law granted by the Australian legal system does not end any enquiry about the existence of Indigenous law, which has an independent cultural

---

19 Griffiths (n 2) 2.
20 Anne Griffiths, 'Legal Pluralism' in Reza Banakar and Max Travers (eds), *An Introduction to Law and Social Theory* (Hart 2002) 289, 302.
21 Palmer and Zhou (n 1) 1.
22 Griffiths (n 20) 303.

18 The Conceptual Development of Legal Pluralism

basis. Strong legal pluralism acknowledges not only a normative difference which is accommodated by the mainstream legal system, but also a difference which is independent of and uncontrolled by, dominant law.[23]

Significantly, this bold and untethered 'new' or 'strong' understanding of legal pluralism came to be premised upon an extremely expansive notion of law itself, effectively including within its definition a range of normative ordering that went well beyond even the highly inclusive approach we adopt later in this text. Law, on this account, encompassed everything from wholly informal modes of social control, such as social conventions concerning good manners, to highly formalised institutionalised practices such as the internal normative structures of companies, trade unions, and of states themselves. Such a conceptual shift forces us to consider what attracts the label and quality of 'law' and on what grounds: as Merry says of this new perspective, it investigates 'the ways social groups conceive of ordering, of social relationships, and of ways of determining truth and justice'.[24]

This expansive a conception of law and legality is not without its drawbacks, however. The foundational legal pluralist assertion that there is no state monopoly on law[25] raises what we hereafter call 'The Law Question', which is to say:

> Why is it so difficult to find a word for nonstate law? It is clearly difficult to define and circumscribe these forms of ordering. Where do we stop speaking of law and find ourselves simply describing social life? Is it useful to call all these forms of ordering law? In writing about legal pluralism, I find that once legal centralism has been vanquished, calling all forms of ordering that are not state law by the term law confounds the analysis.[26]

Tamanaha provides a lengthy and somewhat vexed exemplification of this conundrum, pointing out that:

> non-state legal orders range from pockets within state legal systems where indigenous norms and institutions continue to exert social control, to the rule-making and enforcing power of social institutions like corporations or universities, to the normative order that exists

23 Davies (n 15) 93.
24 Merry (n 16) 889.
25 Brian Z Tamanaha, 'The Folly of the Social Scientific Concept of Legal Pluralism' (1993) 20(2) Journal of Law and Society 192, 193.
26 Merry (n 16) 878.

within small social groups, from community associations to little league baseball, down to and including even the family.[27]

This statement is not uncontroversial, and, in our view at least, it is also potentially quite problematic in moral and political terms. This holds because the sort of conceptual elision of different non-state normative orders that Tamanaha suggests in the quoted passage often leads in practice to the reemergence of legal centralism by other means. In particular, it places Indigenous legal orders at risk of being once more denied the status of 'law' on the basis of the unwarranted assumption that, by virtue of their 'non-state' nature, they must have something fundamentally in common with the rules of clubs or the internal norms of families, to which it may well stretch both credulity and good sense to apply the moniker 'legal'. Crucially, as we argue at length in Chapter 2, such denials of status in relation to Indigenous legal orders are not merely academic. Their outcome is almost always the suppression of Indigenous legal orders as means for collective self-determination via the 'marginalisation and suppression [of such orders] as "mere" customary or traditional practices'.[28] Notwithstanding these troubling implications, Tamanaha nevertheless puts his finger on a central issue for legal pluralists to ponder: in circumstances where law is *not* coupled directly to the state, how can this definitionally 'lower conceptual status'[29] – 'only' social rules, *mere* informal practices – be avoided?[30]

Although legal anthropologists and legal sociologists continued to wrangle with The Law Question, this key query about the nature and character of law under circumstances of plurality served to attract the attention of different scholars in the legal academy, including analytical legal philosophers – specifically, the legal positivists. As Davies observed, 'the assumption that it is possible to find a conceptual distinction between things that are law and things that are not has . . . characterised (indeed defined) legal positivism'.[31] Legal positivist efforts to provide a conceptually satisfactory solution to The Law Question were of an essentially descriptive nature, helping to earn them the label 'social fact legal pluralism'.

---

27 Tamanaha (n 25) 193.
28 Alex Green and Jennifer Hendry, 'Non-Positivist Legal Pluralism and Crises of Legitimacy in Settler-States' (2019) 14(2) Journal of Comparative Law 267, 271.
29 Franz von Benda-Beckmann, 'Legal Pluralism and Social Justice in Economic and Political Development' (2001) 32(1) IDS Bulletin 46, 48.
30 Interestingly, Davies's 2018 methodological point of departure is to set 'aside Merry's anxiety over where law stops and where social normativity starts', on the grounds that this fixation 'unduly limits legal theory to questions of definition, and prevents an expansive and experimental approach to understanding law's multiplicity'. See Davies (n 7) 40, and also section 7 of this chapter.
31 ibid 39.

4. Social Fact Legal Pluralism

This name derives from the twin legal positivist propositions known as the 'separation thesis' and the 'social source thesis'. Excepting certain nuances, the first holds there to be a strict separation between, on the one hand, the question of what the content of the law on any given matter in fact is and, on the other, the (allegedly) distinct question of how the content of that same law ought to be. The second holds, once again excepting some nuance, that the existence of law is fundamentally a matter of *social fact* because the validity of any given set of legal norms turns either ultimately or exclusively on their social sources and not their normative merits.[32]

When understood in this manner, some version of legal positivism almost certainly sits philosophically upstream from every conception of legal pluralism so far discussed within this chapter. Anthropological and sociological understandings of law, even those that are avowedly against any kind of legal centralism are, in this limited sense, all positivist theories. However, it was only when positivist legal philosophers themselves began to engage with the question of legal pluralism directly that this fact became clear. Perhaps more interestingly for present purposes, the development of social fact legal pluralism by these philosophers also resulted in the development of some really rather radical enclaves within positivist legal philosophy itself. In a deliberately controversial move, for example, Tamanaha provides an unsparingly stripped-back version of HLA Hart's traditionally centralist conception of law,[33] which retains only what Tamanaha considers to be the most essential premise of legal positivism, namely that '[l]aw is whatever people identify and treat through their social practices as law'.[34] On this understanding, 'law can be said to exist even if it has no functions, is ineffective, has no institutions or enforcement, involves no union of primary and secondary rules, and even if there is no normative element', concluding that these minimal identifying criteria allow Tamanaha to embrace, under a single conception of law: 'state law, customary law, religious law, international law, transnational law, and even natural law (secular as well as religious)', on the grounds that these are all 'social products', the existence of which is a *matter of social fact*.[35] Therefore, at its broadest and most inclusive, social fact legal pluralism can be said to oppose state centralism, to accept the premise of non-state law, and to have a distinctively empirical bent, notwithstanding its roots within legal philosophy.

---

32 For an excellent discussion of the essential features of legal positivism, see John Gardener, 'Legal Positivism: 5½ Myths' (2001) 46 American Journal of Jurisprudence 199.
33 William Twining, *General Jurisprudence* (CUP 2009) 93–95.
34 Brian Z Tamanaha, *A General Jurisprudence of Law and Society* (OUP 2001) 166, 194.
35 Twining (n 33) 95, quoting Tamanaha, ibid 159.

It is worth briefly contrasting Tamanaha's position with Hart's own so the degree of his departure can be properly apprehended. For Hart, law is a union of primary social rules, which directly govern individual behaviour, and secondary social rules, which govern the existence and application of the former.[36] At the apex of any given legal order, Hart locates a single rule of recognition, a social convention which exists as a coincidence of attitude and behaviour amongst law-applying officials.[37] This 'master rule' provides criteria for legal validity that determine which primary and secondary rules form part of the overall system.[38] Stated in such abstract terms, it might seem as though Hart would have no difficulty accepting the possibility of legal pluralism across quite a broad set of circumstances. All that would be necessary for legal pluralism would be for two or more discrete rules of recognition to exist in relation to the practices of two or more sets of law-applying officials, each of which practiced these distinct and respective social conventions in relation to just one shared social space. For those who accept Hart's schema, the historical relation between law and equity within England and Wales, prior to the Judicatur Acts of 1873 and 1875, may well provide one key example. Nonetheless, even notions as abstract as a union of primary and secondary rules, together with shared official criteria for legal validity, can be highly exclusionary when compared to Tamanaha's permissive approach. Hart himself described normative orders without a rule of recognition (and other rules providing for mechanisms of legal change and official adjudication) as mere 'custom' belonging to 'primitive societies'.[39] Leaving aside for the moment the racist connotations of this language, Hart's insistence upon the basic systematicity of law and the requirement that it be capable of governing large and impersonal societies efficiently quite clearly smacks of legal centralism.[40]

Tamanaha's fundamentally empirical and linguistic turn is, by contrast, wildly permissive: indeed, Franz von Benda-Beckmann presents the position endorsed by Tamanaha as the preferred one of many legal anthropologists and legal sociologists, largely on the grounds of its clear break with the state/law nexus. He explains this alternative as a means through which:

> to conceive of law analytically by a set of properties in a way in which the exclusive connection to the state organisation is given up, and other organisational structures and sources of validity, such as old or

---

36 HLA Hart, *The Concept of Law* (3rd edn, OUP 2015) 81.
37 ibid 101–3.
38 ibid 100.
39 ibid 91.
40 ibid 92–99.

invented traditions or religion, can match the analytical properties of the concept. [. . .] Law is then defined independently from the way in which state legal systems define it and the respective spheres of validity of non-state normative orders.[41]

The consequences of Tamanaha embracing such an inclusive conception of social fact legal pluralism are worth emphasising, not least because his focus on the empirically oriented and descriptive identification of non-state normative orders means that social fact legal pluralism does not concern itself over much with 'normative questions about legitimacy, authority, justification, obligatoriness, and official policies toward non-state normative orders and laws'.[42] Much like more traditional legal positivist accounts along the lines of Hart's own, social fact legal pluralism pays scant attention to normative issues, with the result that its guidance on such questions is negligible. Our own approach, developed in Chapters 2 and 3, is methodologically as far from this purely descriptive endeavour as it is possible to be. Indeed, it is partly in the hope of providing the kind of normative guidance that social fact legal pluralism cannot that we adopt a fundamentally *non-positivist* conception of legal plurality.

Another key feature of social fact legal pluralism worth highlighting here is its apparently strategic shift from the language of legal pluralism to what William Twining and others call 'normative pluralism'.[43] Normative pluralism of this kind is not to be confused with an appeal to the kind of critical normativity that we rely upon in Chapters 2 and 3. At bottom, it represents a fundamentally positivist shift away from the language of law and towards the language of *social* normativity, and provides another way of addressing The Law Question. As we discuss earlier, this essentially definitional concern relates to what can be done about the distortive broadening of the category of 'the legal' invoked by the inclusion of non-state forms of normative ordering. This conceptual distinction between law and non-law was, as we have seen, the source of considerable controversy, and it is perhaps telling that, in response, positivist philosophers interested in the phenomenon of legal pluralism have been tempted towards jettisoning the language of 'law' altogether.

Interestingly, perhaps the most prominent scholar to switch to the normative pluralist viewpoint after its introduction was John Griffiths.

---

41 Von Benda-Beckmann (n 29) 48.

42 'Insofar as [social fact legal pluralism] studies have been largely descriptive rather than normative, one should not expect much practical normative guidance about such issues as institutional design, state policy, or rights-based approaches to development'. William Twining, 'Normative and Legal Pluralism: A Global Perspective' (2010) 20 Duke Journal of Comparative and International Law 473, 516.

43 ibid.

In 2005, '[a]fter two decades of forcefully promoting the notion of legal pluralism',[44] Griffiths proclaimed that:

> further reflection on the concept of law has led me to the conclusion that the 'law' could be better abandoned altogether for the purposes of theory formation in sociology of law [. . . . and that it] follows from the above considerations that the expression 'legal pluralism' can and should be reconceptualized as 'normative pluralism' or 'pluralism in social control'.[45]

Proponents of *normative* pluralism are thus of the view that it is generally preferable to reject legal pluralism as an overly inclusive classification in relation to the concept of law instead of simply having to accept the 'loss of distinction between the law and other social rules, such as customs, practices and morals'.[46] Twining's own normative pluralism arose from his fundamental position that this law/non-law issue was either ancillary to or redundant for most empirical investigations: allowing for the provision that those 'phenomena designated as unofficial law or non-state law or law-like normative orders deserve our attention as jurists as an essential part of understanding law',[47] little is practically at stake. It is for this reason that he was generally of the view that the obsession with 'where to draw the line between legal and non-legal phenomena'[48] – the 'definitional stop', as he puts it – was entirely overblown.

On the other hand, Tamanaha, whose antagonism to the 'legal' in legal pluralism really always placed him in the normative pluralist camp,[49] has both welcomed and praised Griffiths's *volte face*.[50] Cleaving to the social facticity of normative pluralism, Tamanaha introduces the term 'folk law' to encompass 'what people in each context examined conventionally identify as law',[51] explaining further that, importantly, 'what counts as law is what communities identify as law (and its translations)'.[52] Such social facts include the governance practices

---

44 Brian Z Tamanaha, 'Scientific v Folk Legal Pluralism' (2021) 53(3) Journal of Legal Pluralism and Unofficial Law 434.
45 John Griffiths, 'The Idea of Sociology of Law and Its Relation to Law and to Sociology' (2005) 8 Current Legal Issues 49, 63–64.
46 Jennifer Hendry, 'Legal Pluralism and Normative Transfer' in Günter Frankenberg (ed), *Order from Transfer: Comparative Constitutional Design and Legal Culture* (Edward Elgar 2013) 153, 165.
47 Twining (n 42) 497.
48 ibid.
49 Tamanaha (n 25) generally.
50 Tamanaha (n 44) 434.
51 ibid 435.
52 ibid 428.

24 The Conceptual Development of Legal Pluralism

used by communities to organise their collective lives,[53] in a manner that Melissaris has described as stemming from 'the shared belief of participants in a *nomos* in transforming the world normatively and in common', which is to say, according to 'our *prima facie* sense of the law'.[54] Merry encapsulates the prevalent legal anthropological position on this issue, which is that '[s]ince the focus of legal pluralist analysis is on connections, exchanges, conflicts, and assertions of power among legal regimes, the general tendency is to adopt an *expansive* conception of law'.[55] Importantly, and in clear contradistinction to the legal aesthetics of state centralism, such legally pluralist conceptions have no underpinning requirement for coherence or consistency – if anything, they lean into the fragmentations and contradictions engendered by that plurality, by and through localised, situated, material normative practices. Although we appreciate the instrumental anthropological and sociological utility of such definitional flexibility, for the reasons canvassed in the previous subsection and developed more fully in Chapter 2, we are highly sceptical of any attempt *by legal philosophers* to reduce The Law Question to one of mere semantics. In our view, what counts as law in conceptual terms matters both morally and politically, such that the problematic nature of Hart's centralist positivism lies in its exclusionary nature rather than in its search for conceptual clarity as such.

5. Interlegality and Legal Pluralism

At this stage of our discussion of legal pluralism's conceptual development, it is useful to pause and take stock. What we have outlined so far is that legal pluralism – which is the term we will continue to use – is the view that law exists not only within and relation to the formal, official institutions of the state but also in everyday life, in various sites, and across multiple normative traditions. Initially conceived of as an explanatory device for the discussion of imposed law in colonial and postcolonial situations, the conceptual difficulties generated, first, by state recognition requirements (its weak or classic form) and subsequently by The Law Question resulted in an expansive, bottom-up, practically oriented, and fundamentally descriptive understanding, one that 'emphasizes the multiplicity of law and the fuzzy boundaries between law and social life'.[56]

---

53 Green and Hendry (n 28) 270.
54 Emmanuel Melissaris *Ubiquitous Law: Legal Theory and the Space for Legal Pluralism* (Routledge 2009) 112.
55 Sally Engle Merry, 'An Anthropological Perspective on Legal Pluralism' in Paul Schiff Berman (ed), *The Oxford Handbook of Global Legal Pluralism* (OUP 2020) 169.
56 ibid.

The Conceptual Development of Legal Pluralism 25

It is to this multiplicity of law that our attention now turns and to what has been called the 'phenomenological counterpart of pluralism', *interlegality*.[57] Coined by Boaventura de Sousa Santos, interlegality is 'the conception of different legal spaces superimposed, interpenetrated, and mixed in our minds as much in our actions . . . Our legal life is constituted by [this] intersection of different legal orders'.[58] This conception effectively turns on the idea of legal orders' interaction and interrelation, in notable distinction to the earlier notion that co-existing legal orders were necessarily oppositional, that is, that they either competed or conflicted. Twining draws our attention to this apparent descriptive error, writing that:

> the possible kinds of relations between co-existing legal orders can be extraordinarily diverse: they may complement each other; the relationship may be one of co-operation, co-optation, competition, subordination, or stable symbiosis; the orders may converge, assimilate, merge, repress, imitate, echo, or avoid each other.[59]

Instead of subsisting in circumstances of constant and intractable conflict – which, when you think about it, would be extremely impractical – therefore, in practice, substantial elements of law as we experience it are shaped, influenced, and moulded by the complex interactions of different legal orders, regulating and controlling various aspects of social life at different levels and scales of social organisation.

It is by means of a meditation on 'legal scale', in the sense of law's spatial and geographical scope, that Santos elucidates his interactional conception of interlegality. In fact, scale is so central to his thinking in this vein that he takes the view that to overlook scalar considerations is to miss entirely those key regulation patterns, power dynamics, and complex social relationships at play amongst and across them. Observing that 'legal developments reveal the existence of three different legal spaces and their corresponding forms of law: local, national, and world legality',[60] Santos makes the case that these legal spaces need governance systems *specific* to their scale. Dividing the legal world into three broadly described scales – the local, the national, and the international or global, as noted – he draws our attention to how the same *social*

---

57 Boaventura de Sousa Santos, 'Law: A Map of Misreading. Toward a Postmodern Conception of Law' (1987) 14(3) Journal of Law and Society 279, 297–98.

58 ibid. Phenomenology, in crude terms, is the study of structures of consciousness from the perspective of first person experience. See David Smith, 'Phenomenology' in Edward Zalta (ed), *The Stanford Encyclopedia of Philosophy* (2018) <https://plato.stanford.edu/archives/sum2018/entries/phenomenology/> last accessed 7 April 2024.

59 Twining (n 33) 277.

60 Santos (n 57) 287.

26 The Conceptual Development of Legal Pluralism

objects can be different *legal* objects at different scales of legality. His own explanation here is worth quoting at length:

> Let us assume that local law is a *large-scale legality*, nation-state law, a *medium-scale legality*, and global law, a *small-scale legality*. This means, first of all, that since scale creates the phenomenon, the different forms of law create different legal objects upon the same social objects. In other words, laws use different criteria to determine the meaningful details and the relevant features of the activity to be regulated, that is to say, they establish different networks of facts. In sum, different forms of law create different legal realities.[61]

While it would be correct to identify the medium scale, nation-state legality as being a state centralist one, the other two legalities mentioned here by Santos, local and global, are characterised by an expansive understanding of law, and one broadly in keeping with the non-state, legally pluralist conceptions discussed previously.[62] Some proponents of interlegality go even further, contending that limiting our view to only the three scales suggested by Santos has the effect of obscuring other salient scales. Valverde in particular criticises this tripartite scalar differentiation as a limited and overly simplistic articulation of a much larger phenomenon of legal interrelatedness, scope, and extent.[63] Be that as it may, it is sufficient here to take the point that social life, for Santos, is 'constituted by different legal spaces operating simultaneously on different scales and from different interpretive standpoints'.[64]

One important thing to notice about this perspective is that it brings to the fore the immense complexity of legal orders in constant interaction, impacting upon, refining, and redefining each other through all this activity. Several points can be made in relation to this observation. First, in the intricate and interdependent circumstances of interlegality, local, national, and global scales are neither self-contained nor autonomous: as Davies explains, these scales 'overlap and interact in various ways, for instance by the selective borrowing of state law concepts by the informal local legal processes'.[65] To quote Santos yet again: 'We live in a time of porous legality or of legal porosity, of multiple networks of legal orders forcing us

---

61 Boaventura de Sousa Santos, *Towards A New Legal Common Sense* (Sweet and Maxwell 2002) 40.
62 Davies (n 7) 100.
63 Mariana Valverde, *Chronotopes of Law* (Routledge Glasshouse 2015) 59.
64 Santos (n 57) 288.
65 Davies (n 7) 99.

The Conceptual Development of Legal Pluralism   27

to constant transitions and trespassings';[66] such legal porosity can be considered as very far-removed from the ordered neatness of both more traditional analytical legal philosophy and the fundamentally modernist legal aesthetic of state centralism.

Second, precisely because this 'interlegal' complexity creates different legal realities across different scales and spaces, it also creates choices for legal subjects. Merry makes this point in terms of power, observing that such 'interactions reveal the relative power balance among legal spheres. Power is exercised when one system or order trumps the decision of others. Individuals may be able to *choose* among these multiple orders, either in sequence or simultaneously, in a creative way'.[67] Although this might be overstating the degree of choice experienced by different individuals in different circumstances (the degree of manoeuvrability available to actors in this regard depends respectively on their social, economic, and political power)[68] and while this aspect of agency can also be overlooked, it is a key descriptive point:

> [The global, national, and local spaces defining these different scales of law] are constituted . . . by spatio-temporal engagements and by the movement of people between systems that are differentiated in theory and practice, but that are also entangled by virtue of the human agents moving between them.[69]

Third and finally, by identifying and recasting such legal complexity, the perspective of interlegality provided both inspiration and theoretical foundations for several other explanatory conceptual tools within an increasingly voluminous literature on legal pluralism, including the concepts of 'polycentrism, . . . parallel legal orders, nomosphere, hybridity, vernacularization, iterations, law fare, [and] legal diversity'.[70] We cannot hope to do every such concept proper justice here; for present purposes, it suffices to note that as legal pluralism became more popular, more controversial, more diverse, and more generally accepted as an object for serious and interdisciplinary academic study, interlegality itself became a nexus for multiperspectival analysis.

We conclude this section by moving from interlegality as such to Santos's own conception of legal pluralism (although these last words are not his own but rather Melissaris's). Santos's legal pluralism is 'the new reality in which we develop new ways of understanding the world

66 Santos (n 57) 298.
67 Merry (n 55) 170, emphasis added.
68 Von Benda-Beckmann (n 13) 68.
69 Davies (n 7) 99.
70 Von Benda-Beckmann and Turner (n 4) 265.

28 The Conceptual Development of Legal Pluralism

and therefore new ways of regulating our lives. However, this regulation is not static, it does not and cannot claim finality. It is an ongoing process of rediscovering and regulating the world'.[71] In the same spirit, interlegality itself can thus be understood as 'a cluster of interpenetrating legalities, which regulate all instances of our whole lives and correspond to our knowledge of the world'.[72] Such knowledge is integral to the regulation we experience, as is our positionality, in the sense of our location within complex and interacting social identities such as race, class, gender, and geographical location. The next section takes up this last point by considering legal pluralism in terms of non-Western and Global South conceptions.

6. Legal Pluralism From Non-Western and Global South Perspectives

Comparative law's theoretical literature has long featured arguments for 'recognising the inherent plurality of law',[73] although such arguments often struggled for purchase in the face of a universalising logic particular to (modern) Western law and legal thought. Legal comparatist Patrick Glenn draws our attention to how, while all the major legal traditions have 'achieve[d] complexity because of their proven ability to hold together mutually inconsistent sub-traditions' (the previously discussed 'messy compromise') the Western world is conspicuous in its fierce defence of its own 'bivalent logical constructions'.[74] What he identifies here is the manner in which the modern Western legal tradition hid away its innate diversity while pushing to the fore its ostensible unity and uniformity. This homogenising drive is especially interesting when cast in historical light, for, as MacDonald explains:

> Until the seventeenth century in Europe the idea of a territorial State . . . claiming an exclusive capacity to regulate everyday activity would have been thought bizarre. Neither the Romans (with, *inter alia*, their conceptions of *jus civile* and *jus gentium*) nor the medieval kings of England (who tolerated both customary law of the realm and of localities, and divergent manorial, ecclesiastical and mercantile legal systems) claimed a monopoly on law and normativity. What is

71 Emmanuel Melissaris, 'The More the Merrier? A New Take on Legal Pluralism' (2004) 13(1) Social & Legal Studies 63. This idea notably foreshadows the *critical* legal pluralist idea of law as a process; see section 7.

72 ibid 65.

73 Werner Menski, *Comparative Law in a Global Context: Legal Systems of Africa and Asia* (2nd ed, CUP 2006) 26. Menski also highlights notable differences between Western/non-Western law as being their respective treatment of religious law, and of collective action as opposed to individual agency, ibid 32.

74 H Patrick Glenn, *Legal Traditions of the World* (OUP 2004) 349–51.

more, even into the nineteenth century, the legal and political *elites* of England and France, for example, did not see law as singular. That is, only with codification on the continent and with the *Judicature Acts* in common law jurisdictions did the image of a single, State-managed legal system being to emerge.[75]

This Western, and arguably also Global North, image of law is underpinned by three key and interrelated premises: first, the aesthetic preference for legal theoretical coherence; second, the 'universalising nature of traditional jurisprudence';[76] and third, the spatially hegemonic claim of formal or official (which is to say, typically *state*) law. This first point was discussed at length in Section 2, but the latter two deserve some additional attention. The secular, Western state is a particular beneficiary of analytical legal philosophy's (especially legal formalist and legal positivist)[77] claims to universality. Thus aided and abetted, modern Western law, in conception and constellation, was able to present itself as neutral, general, and culturally unspecific in terms of both pedigree and practice. There is power in such assertions of atemporality and universality, not least the claim to superiority, whether they are uttered explicitly or 'merely' implicit and assumed. Chiba's observation in this regard is pertinent:

> [C]ontemporary model jurisprudence is a product of long Western history and is coloured by a Western culture based on the Hellenistic and Christian view of man and society. While we acknowledge the universalistic achievements of Western jurisprudence as the most advanced science of law ever accomplished by man, *we cannot disregard its cultural specificity.*[78]

Importantly, far from being some wholly objective realisation or reified ideal image, Western legal thought and practice are as culturally determined and historically contingent as non-Western legal conceptions and forms. Recognising this cannot justify us dismissing the insights of

---

75 Roderick A MacDonald, 'Metaphors of Multiplicity: Civil Society, Regimes, and Legal Pluralism' (1998) 15 Arizona Journal of International and Comparative Law 74–75.

76 Masaji Chiba, 'Introduction' in Masaji Chiba (ed), *Asian Indigenous Law* (Routledge 1986) 1.

77 Ugo Mattei actually elides legal positivism with legal formalism: '[L]egal positivism is the enemy of understanding in the law. It is a reductionist perspective that artificially excludes from the picture the deeper structure of law . . . [and is], as a consequence . . . unmasked as an inherently formalistic approach, in the sense that form prevails over structure in determining law's domain'. See Ugo Mattei, 'The Comparative Jurisprudence of Schlesinger and Sacco: A Study in Legal Influence' in Annelise Riles (ed), *Rethinking the Masters of Comparative Law* (Hart Bloomsbury 2001) 254.

78 Chiba (n 76) 2, emphasis added.

analytical legal philosophy out of hand. However, it should prevent us from taking many of the arguments raised within it entirely at face value, a point which takes us neatly to Western law's hegemonic claim: one that must already appear at least presumptively weakened in the light of its recognised contingency. This claim rests on the 'formal' idea of law as, to quote Desmond Manderson, 'a domain [that] organises relationships, abstractly and entirely, over a legal territory'.[79] Manderson continues by noting that, under legal formalism, 'judgments of law have no temporal dimension, no history, no social context or evolution. Rather "the law" is understood to exist all at once, organising principles over a space that law unproblematically and exclusively controls'.[80] Much of the conceptual utility of legal pluralism, we would argue, lies in the challenge it helps pose to such overriding, totalising narratives that operate so as wrongfully to exclude normative practices properly considered legal notwithstanding their undeniable cultural, historical, and social contingency.

In discussing and exposing Western legal ethnocentricity, then, it is useful to ponder those assumptions that influenced contemporary legal and normative (in Twining's sense) pluralist conceptions. One unpleasant modern 'evolutionist' rationality in fact relied upon the 'actual plurality in the field of law' in order to compile a presumptive hierarchy of legal orders, effectively distinguishing on *developmental* grounds between Western legal order frontrunners and non-Western dawdlers. Particularly obvious in the work of those such as Hart, discussed earlier, the problematic premise here is that, where 'some societies are progressing faster than others – the stragglers represent . . . the earlier stage of development through which the leaders have long passed'.[81] This 'developed' as opposed to 'un(der)developed' distinction between legal orders is, of course, culturally partisan nonsense (and both a dangerous and racist nonsense at that). Indeed, it was hegemonic and colonial thinking of precisely this kind that underpinned the state centralist politics of 'weak' legal pluralism so derided by John Griffiths, and served to facilitate the unjust and bigoted dismissal of, amongst other things, tribal and Indigenous legal orders. Thankfully, there has been robust recent pushback against this view within legal pluralism scholarship, with a concerted drive towards understanding legal diversity not as a 'temporary intermediate stage in the evolution of law toward unified systems' but as

---

79 Desmond Manderson, 'Beyond the Provincial: Space, Aesthetics, and Modernist Legal Theory' (1996) 20 Melbourne LR 1048, 1054.

80 ibid.

81 Menski (n 73) 26, quoting Peter Sack and Jonathan Aleck, *Law and Anthropology* (NYU Press 1992) xviii–xix.

'distinct, enduring, socio-legal arrangements here to stay owing to deep historical, social, cultural, economic, political, and legal factors'.[82]

Theories concerning this presumed hierarchy of legal orders also crop up in comparative law, where much of the (albeit now largely discredited) discourse on legal transplants presented Western systems as the donors of complete and *completed* legal features, institutions, and practices.[83] Chiba calls out this backhanded conceptualisation of cross-cultural legal change, noting how central consideration within the very notion of legal transplants 'is given to the destiny of the received Western law rather than to the receiving indigenous systems'.[84] Frankenberg is similarly disapproving of this notion and criticises Alan Watson's 'formula' of '[b]orrowing plus adaptation' as representative of "the usual way of legal development".[85] The assumption that customary, tribal, Indigenous, and social law was somehow inferior ('minor law', as Chiba terms it)[86] is now generally rejected by legal pluralists.

Finally, and sticking with what has, historically, fallen within the ambit of comparative law, attention must be paid not just to borrowed but rather to *imposed* law and its attendant issues of power. Law imposed by foreign powers, in both colonial and other settings, not only claimed hierarchical superiority – for illustration of this, one need only reflect on the traditional comparative law notion of 'parent' legal systems[87] – but also presented and established itself as culturally neutral and objective and, through this symbiosis, functioned 'both as the foundation and the mask for a variety of structural violence and persistent inequality'.[88] As Duthu notes, 'the study of legal pluralism in the context of colonial societies and the attendant encounters between Indigenous peoples and European imperialists are particularly attentive to and concerned with the interactions of these respective legal systems in conditions of grossly unequal power'.[89]

---

82 Brian Z Tamanaha, 'Legal Pluralism Across the Global South: Colonial Origins and Contemporary Consequences' (2021) 53(2) Journal of Legal Pluralism and Unofficial Law 168.

83 See Alan Watson, *Legal Transplants. An Approach to Comparative Law* (Scottish Academic Press 1974).

84 Chiba (n 76) 5.

85 Günter Frankenberg, 'Constitutional Transfer: The IKEA Theory Revisited' (2010) 8(3) I-CON 563, 567, quoting Watson ibid 7.

86 Masaji Chiba, 'Other Phases of Legal Pluralism in the Contemporary World' (1998) 11(3) Ratio Juris 228, 229.

87 See for example Twining (n 33) 283–84, and Konrad Zweigert and Hein Kötz, *An Introduction to Comparative Law* (Tony Weir tr, 3rd edn, OUP 1998) 40–41.

88 Jennifer Hendry, 'A Legal Pluralist Approach to the Bakassi Peninsula Case' in Damien Gonzalez-Salzberg and Loveday Hudson (eds), *Research Methods for International Human Rights Law: Beyond the Traditional Paradigm* (Routledge 2019) 123, 127–28.

89 N Bruce Duthu, *Shadow Nations: Tribal Sovereignty and the Limits of Legal Pluralism* (OUP 2013) 11.

32 The Conceptual Development of Legal Pluralism

Nowhere is the violence of this power asymmetry more apparent than in Irene Watson's unflinching account of imposed law in circumstances of colonisation: '[f]rom the attempted genocide of Nungas (Aboriginal peoples) the Australian state retains control over Nunga territory, the ruwi (land) of my ancestors, through a power which mantles a white Australian homogenous identity, over our Nunganess'.[90] She continues:

> [N]ow *terra nullius* is 'known' to be dead – [the question is:] what constitutes the state? The question is met with a silence of an unrecognised violence – a power of the state to annihilate all that is different. Without answering the question the state offers a process of reconciliation, one which leaves intact the scars of annihilation, one which refuses to give restitution for the loss of country, and life, as it continues to bore even deeper into the earth and the Nunga being.[91]

It is this violently universalising quality of colonising state law that our own argument for 'non-positivist' legal pluralism in Chapters 2 and 3 sets itself against. Our concern, in a nutshell, is that it is morally and politically insufficient to point in descriptive terms to a plurality of normative orders and then to leave matters there. Unless one is prepared vigorously to defend particular non-state normative orders as distinctively and importantly legal in conceptual and normative terms, one is liable quietly to license hegemonic state centralism by virtue of what one either refuses or has neglected to say. On this basis, we would amend Santos's famous declaration to read that there is 'nothing inherently good, progressive or emancipatory about [*descriptive*] legal pluralism'.[92]

7. Critical Legal Pluralism and Our Point of Departure

Recent years have seen an emerging body of critical scholarship on legal pluralism. 'Critical legal pluralism', according to Davies, can essentially be understood as the 'effort to amalgamate the critique of foundations, sources, and closure with socio-legal insights about the material plurality of legal forms'.[93] The unifying characteristics of such critical approaches lie in how they employ both bottom-up and dynamic conceptualisations of law and legal processes to identify plural legalities not only where different legal orders exist within one territory but also to situate pluralism within both 'the very nature of law' and those 'social and political

---

90 Irene Watson, 'Buried Alive' (2002) 13 Law and Critique 253, 254.
91 ibid 265.
92 Santos (n 61) 114–15.
93 Davies (n 7) 33.

The Conceptual Development of Legal Pluralism   33

dialogues that are constitutive of law'.[94] The conception of law needed to facilitate such approaches is necessarily an ecumenical one, although how this is handled by different scholars within the critical tradition naturally admits considerable variation. Davies herself calls her own radical and expansive approach 'unlimited', in that it is 'open-ended, interpretable, in flux, formed by everyday relations, and contextual. [Law] is both personal and dialogical; it is practised and reduced (albeit contingently) to a finite form. It thus occurs subjectively, as well as inter-subjectively, and interculturally'.[95] The key conceptual accommodation undertaken by critical legal pluralists is one of legal pluralism as an undetermined process, an ongoing dynamic engagement with existing and potential normative practices through which 'what is regarded as law' is continuously created, evaluated, refined, and transformed.[96] The relationship between this kind of radical philosophical project and our own non-positivist approach makes for an interesting contrast. We share Davies's belief that pluralism must be accommodated within any inter-pretively sound conception of the nature of law, and insofar as we also believe that nature to be at least partly practice-driven, we share the con-viction that the concept of law itself may well alter through time as the relevant practices change. However, the accounts of both law and legal pluralism developed in Chapters 2 and 3 differ from Davies in believing that the nature of law ultimately turns on subjective, intersubjective, and intercultural facts alone. Instead, we make several (admittedly con-troversial) arguments about genuine practical reasons – those consid-erations that truly, and perhaps even in a mind-independent manner, determine how we should behave at the individual, interpersonal, and collective social and political levels.[97] We believe the nature of law (capi-tal 'L', as it were) to admit legal pluralism because law as it exists within our contemporary world is ultimately an inclusive moral and political concept, even though we do not understand it to be either as contingent or as fundamentally in flux as Davies suggests.

As we have observed elsewhere, Davies's 'critical legal pluralism is the pluralism *of pluralism*: not just a vein of legal pluralism but a variety of legal theory, an approach specifically intended 'to debunk the idea that there is either an objective or true version of legal pluralism"'.[98] Impor-tantly, and for this very reason, this critical project of legal pluralism is, in addition to being a discrete and complex philosophical approach,

94   ibid.
95   ibid 34.
96   ibid 119. See also Kirsten Anker, *Declarations of Interdependence* (Ashgate 2014) 187.
97   For the notion of a genuine practical reason, see: Derek Parfit, *On What Matters*, vol 1 (OUP 2011) 31. For a useful discussion of 'mind-independence' and its relation to sub-jectivity, see: Matthew Kramer, *Objectivity and the Rule of Law* (CUP 2007) 3–14.
98   Green and Hendry (n 28) 273.

also *a moral and political project* aimed at rendering the concept and the study of law far more inclusive than has traditionally been the case within both analytical legal philosophy and a great deal of more empirically-minded legal scholarship. Notably, this marks it as different in terms of both ambition and scope from many of the more descriptive approaches previously outlined within this chapter and places it in a position of significant ideological convergence with our own non-positivist account of legal pluralism, advanced in Chapters 2 and 3. Although our own methods differ considerably from those adopted by critical legal scholars analysing legal pluralism, based as they are within the very analytical legal philosophy critical scholars characteristically seek to oppose, we share the very same moral and political project that Davies so powerfully articulates within her own work. In the next chapter, we begin advancing this project on our own terms in the hope that much we will say remains true to the spirit of the critical theory that we have both come to so admire.

Chapter 2

The Value(s) of Law and the Possibility of Its Plurality

1. Introduction

As Chapter 1 demonstrated, it is impossible to define 'legal pluralism' in a wholly uncontroversial manner. Scholars writing from different traditions fundamentally disagree, both about how to characterise legal pluralism and about how it should be identified in practice. As such, rather than getting lost in the woods of these ongoing debates, we will make a fresh start and, in so doing, provide a new and important perspective, practically speaking, through which legal pluralities can be understood. This chapter takes the first steps along that path, developing a normative philosophical framework through which the existence of overlapping legal orders can be conceptualised. When presenting this framework, we presume a particular relationship between, on the one hand, the existence of a legal order and, on the other, the instantiation of a distinctive set of political values often referred to as 'the Rule of Law'.[1] Put simply, we take a legal order to exist wherever (and to the extent that) the Rule of Law is instrumental in the governance of political and social relations. This approach is itself controversial as a matter of general legal philosophy. In particular, it stands in marked opposition to the 'legal positivist' idea that the existence of law is purely a matter of social fact, which can be settled in an entirely descriptive manner. Indeed, the understanding of law we employ from this point on explicitly requires contemplation of what philosophers sometimes call 'genuine normative reasons'.[2] These are practical considerations that *actually* determine how particular

---

1 By 'political values' we mean normative concepts that determine how one ought to act in relation to political matters, which encompass not only how societies should be organised at a collective or institutional level but also how we as a species should 'live together', see: Ronald Dworkin, *Justice for Hedgehogs* (Harvard UP 2011) 327–50.
2 Derek Parfit, *On What Matters*, vol 1 (OUP 2011) 31.

DOI: 10.4324/9781003532149-3

36 The Value(s) of Law and the Possibility of Its Plurality

individuals should behave, irrespective of what any person or group might believe about the matter.[3]

To understand this important distinction, imagine that you have promised your friend that you will meet them for coffee tomorrow morning. The fact that you spoke the relevant words is a purely descriptive matter: an event which could have been observed by anyone who happened to pass by at the time. However, that descriptive fact alone cannot explain why your words bind you. Something else is needed to explain the normative potency of the phrase 'I promise': something which cannot be either observed or described.[4] You are bound to meet your friend because you gave them your word. However, your word only has this effect because of something peculiar to promising as a social practice. Crucially, this additional element cannot be either the fact that you *believe* your promise to bind you or even that society as a whole believes that you do. Both of these psychological facts are no less descriptive than the fact that you uttered the phrase 'I promise' when you told your friend you would meet them for coffee. Indeed, no descriptive fact of any sort can explain why (or whether) your promises truly bind you. The additional element required is something quite different: a normative fact about the reason-giving force that promises possess, which explains why promises in general provide genuine normative reasons for keeping them.

Our approach to the existence of law requires engagement with reasons of this sort, albeit less those concerned with promising and more those related to what Fuller calls 'the enterprise of subjecting human conduct to the governance of rules'.[5] Although we accept, as any theorist of law surely must, that every legal order exists as a matter of social reality, we believe that this reality can only be fully comprehended once its normative implications have been properly understood. To that end, this chapter advances an account of law and legal pluralism that draws heavily upon the *value* of law, which, for us, is encapsulated by the concept of the Rule of Law (or 'legality').

This begins in Section 2 with an account of why it is both sensible and important to interrogate the existence of law in the normatively engaged manner just described. Section 3 explains what legality requires in concrete terms, so that its presence within particular social orders can be identified. That move is crucial to our overall framework, for it is the presence or absence of legality as a set of political values upon which our preferred distinction between 'law' and 'not-law' turns. Section 4 then

---

3 For more on this distinction, see: Matthew Kramer, *Objectivity and the Rule of Law* (CUP 2007) 3–14.

4 David Hume, *A Treatise of Human Nature* 3.2.5–14/15–524.

5 Lon Fuller, *The Morality of Law* (Yale UP 1964) 106.

The Value(s) of Law and the Possibility of Its Plurality   37

establishes a philosophical problem: our understanding of legality, with its emphasis upon the subjection of individuals to a single set of governing norms, seems to militate *against* the existence of legal pluralism. After all, how can two legal orders exist in the same social space if the very essence of law lies in its overarching practical authority? Section 5 presents our solution to this problem and, consequently, our preferred means for identifying legal pluralism. Ultimately, we suggest that, in particular social contexts, legality produces an apparent paradox. The very same values that ordinarily mandate societies to organise themselves with reference to a single set of governing norms can, on occasion, mandate that a plurality of governing orders be maintained. In such circumstances, most attempts to dissolve legal pluralism by establishing the ultimate dominance of one order over the other would not only constitute an injustice but also an affront to the normative logic of legality itself. After establishing this framework, Section 6 turns to one important consequence that our account of legality has for the nature of both law and legal pluralism. This is that wherever an independent legal order is established, an important means for collective self-determination is realised. Legality thus has an important positive value: it allows communities of law to exercise agency over their collective destinies. This provides one amongst many other important reasons that law as such, and legal pluralism in particular, must be recognised and respected.

Much of this argument will strike some readers as controversial. In particular, we anticipate some will disagree with our characterisation of the Rule of Law and our understanding of legal pluralism as a fundamentally moral and political phenomenon. However, such controversy is to be celebrated. As the previous chapter demonstrated, universal agreement about legal pluralism is effectively impossible. What matters most is that scholarly accounts of legal pluralism engage with it on the right terms: as a moral and social challenge but also as an opportunity for advancing issues of social justice. By engaging with law as an irreducibly moral phenomenon, we hope to transform arguments over legal pluralism into debates about how our societies should be structured and how past injustices should be addressed.[6] If controversy is inevitable, *these* are the sorts of disagreements we ought to be having.

---

6   In this respect, our approach remains true to the normative commitments of critical legal pluralism, including anti-colonialism and global justice (see Lena Salaymeh, 'Decolonial Translation: Destabilizing Coloniality in Secular Translations of Islamic Law' (2021) 5 Journal of Islamic Ethics 250, 270). Correlatively, insofar as we are pursuing legal philosophy, which we take to be the central component of our overall approach, we are fundamentally opposed to the idea that such philosophy must be either descriptive or focused on what many Western scholars would consider to be the 'ordinary case' (see, for example: Fernanda Pirie, 'Beyond Pluralism: A Descriptive Approach to Non-state Law' (2023) 14(1) Jurisprudence 6–10; Joseph Raz, 'Why the State?' in Nicole Roughan

2. The Constitutive Values and Existence of Law

What might it mean to say that the existence of a legal order is a fundamentally moral and political matter? To those unfamiliar with thinking about law in these terms, the very suggestion might sound absurd. Surely, legal orders exist either as or within things like legislative and adjudicative institutions, authoritative texts, and official practices? This 'plain fact' view of law is widespread, at least within Anglo-American scholarship.[7] There is also, in one very limited and particular sense, something quite uncontroversially true about the intuitions to which this view appeals. No legal order could exist without the kind of social facts that the plain-fact view describes. To exist as law, a normative order must actually govern some kind of human community or at least some significant part of one: it must be, to that extent, minimally 'effective'.[8] No set of principles could constitute law in the total absence of popular compliance, lived experience, or official promulgation, nor could a legal order exist without other important social practices, such as the application of rules, principles, or customs, whatever concrete form that application might take. Although different legal orders vary considerably from each other in both form and structure,[9] they must all possess social facticity of some kind. At bottom, law is something that people *do,* and any competent theory of law must reflect that fact.

Nonetheless, it need not follow from any of this that the plain-fact view is correct. Although particular descriptive facts about human behaviour will always be necessary for the existence of a legal order, this alone cannot entail their sufficiency. True, some scholars believe that social facts of this sort *are* sufficient, going so far as to claim that the concept of law itself entails their sufficiency (and, therefore, that anyone claiming otherwise must be making a conceptual mistake).[10] Within the literature on legal pluralism, beliefs of this 'positivist' sort are most evident in the work of 'social fact' legal pluralists, such as William Twining,[11] although intuitions of a similar kind are arguably also at work elsewhere.[12] Needless to say, we do not share this positivist

---

and Andrew Halpin (eds), *In Pursuit of Pluralist Jurisprudence* (CUP 2017); Muhammad Ali Khalidi and Liam Murphy, 'Disagreement about the Kind of Law' (2020) 12(1) Jurisprudence 1).

7 Ronald Dworkin, *Law's Empire* (Hart Publishing 1998) 7.

8 Hans Kelsen, *General Theory of Law and State* (Anders Wedberg tr, HUP 1961) 42.

9 Cf. Pirie (n 6) 12–14.

10 Joseph Raz, *Ethics and the Public Domain* (OUP 1995) 202.

11 Chapter 1, section 4.

12 For example, the anthropological scholarship that first engaged with legal pluralism is arguably no less focused upon social fact, see: Chapter 1, sections 2 and 3.

commitment. We take the opposite view – that social facts alone are insufficient for the existence of law – and that, as a result, the identification of legal pluralism requires more than an examination of the relevant social facts alone.

This is not the place to rehearse the (rather lengthy) debates between legal positivism and its theoretical opponents. In this section, we have a more modest goal: to show that it is *possible* to understand law in terms of the genuine normative reasons it provides and that this approach is both useful and important. To begin, recall the example of promising that we used at the beginning of this chapter. The reasons that you have to keep your promises belong to a very particular subset of genuine practical reasons. Most obviously, they are distinct from the reasons that apply to your interactions with perfect strangers: those to whom you have made no promise. You might have many reasons to act in particular ways towards strangers – to be polite, to avoid causing offence, to avoid harming them, and so on – but you have no *promissory* reasons in relation to them. Reasons of the latter sort only 'come online' when you make a promise (or have one made to you).[13] In that sense, while promissory reasons are necessary to make normative sense of the phrase 'I promise', the social fact of someone uttering that phrase (or doing something equivalent) is necessary to *engage* the relevant promissory reasons. Promising could not exist without this unique mixture of social and normative fact. Something similar, we suggest, is true of law.

2.1 Law as a Matter of Value

Not every human community is law governed: as Waldron notes, 'to describe an exercise of power as an instance of lawmaking or law application is already to dignify it with a certain character'.[14] Despots who govern by personal decree, issuing orders on an *ad hoc* basis without process or principle, might rule 'effectively' but they do not rule through law, whatever they might claim.[15] As such, whatever reasons one might have to comply with the orders of a despot, whether they are moral or purely instrumental and self-preserving, they cannot be law-related reasons.[16] For legality to influence our normative reasoning, we must belong to or reside within a community in which law, like promising in our

---

13 Promissory reasons are also arguably at work whenever you have the opportunity to mislead someone else, on the assumption that your reasons not to lie and your reasons not to break your promises share similar normative foundations (Dworkin (n 1) 304–10).

14 Jeremy Waldron, 'The Concept and the Rule of Law' (2008) 43(1) Georgia LR 1, 12.

15 Fuller (n 5) 33–94.

16 HLA Hart, *The Concept of Law* (3rd edn, OUP 2012) 82–87.

previous example, has 'come online'. Such a community is one in which the Rule of Law pertains. We explain what this means in more detail in what follows. For now, it is sufficient to understand legality as a particular 'mode of association' between members of the same community,[17] which relies upon their sharing an overarching set of governing customs, principles, or rules. This deliberately capacious understanding of law helps not to exclude the many forms of social order that one might want to consider legal, notwithstanding their divergence from commonly cited Western legal paradigms.

So understood, a community governed by law has a distinct normative character. The predominance of a single set of governing standards entails that each member of the relevant community will be treated as the 'civic' equal of those they live alongside. Such civic equality may not be particularly 'thick' – for instance, contemporary legal orders rarely achieve full socio-economic or gender equality – but it necessarily requires that, in relation to whatever norms govern the community in general, 'there be no "thumb on the scale" for certain individuals we favor'.[18] When someone violates the governing principles of their community without appropriate justification, their actions implicitly disrespect the civic equality that legality establishes. By contrast, when, through compliance, they demonstrate 'faithfulness . . . to each other with respect to some common governing norms',[19] they respect each other *as* civic equals, transforming their common life into what Dworkin describes as 'true' community.[20] Through this process, legality provides us with a distinct set of normative reasons that help to guide our behaviour, even if it does not determine, in an all-things-considered manner, how we should ultimately behave.

2.2 The Existence and Identification of Law

External observers who understand law in this way can identify distinct legal orders through a particular mode of interpretation, which is sometimes referred to as 'rational reconstruction'.[21] To do so, they must examine the practises of the community in question and see whether legality can plausibly be imputed to them. As Dworkin notes, such

---

17 Gerald Postema, 'Fidelity in Law's Commonwealth' in Lisa M Austin and Dennis Klimchuck (eds), *Private Law and the Rule of Law* (OUP 2014) 17.
18 Jeremy Waldron, *One Another's Equals: The Basis of Human Equality* (Belknap Press 2017) 49.
19 Postema (n 17) 37–38.
20 Dworkin (n 7) 201.
21 Jürgen Habermas, *Moral Consciousness and Communicative Action* (Christian Lenhardt and Shierry Weber Nicholson trs, Polity 1990) 31; Alex Green, 'A Political Theory of State Equality' (2023) 14(2) Transnational Legal Theory 178, 188–89.

observers are not looking for 'psychological conditions' (such as actual dispositions or beliefs) but rather 'interpretive propert[ies] of the group's practices'.[22] Moreover, as Habermas emphasises, identifying these properties requires observers to engage in a substantive normative evaluation, meaning that 'the interpreter cannot avoid appealing to standards of rationality and hence to standards that he himself considers binding on all parties'.[23] As such, even those observers who do not participate in the relevant community's practices (and to that extent remain *external*) must become at least moderately *engaged* if they are to identify the presence or absence of law. Since, as we contend, the Rule of Law pertains only insofar as the relevant social practices generate normative reasons of legality, anyone hoping to pronounce upon the presence or absence of law within a given community must be prepared to reach a judgement as to whether its members have genuine reasons to adapt their behaviour in light of the legal practices that exist there.

This interpretive exercise can be hazardous. Exercising engaged judgement in relation to the practices of a community to which one does not belong courts misunderstanding, particularly when that risk is compounded by significant cultural differences.[24] For this reason, an attitude of relative humility must be exercised, informed by an acute awareness of any insufficient cultural embeddedness – and therefore lack of knowledge – on the part of the interpreter. Having said this, since no attempt to evaluate a community other than one's own can be immune to misunderstanding, there is no reason to suppose that engaged interpretation of the sort characterised earlier is *more* prone to mischaracterisation than any other social-scientific approach that does more than merely record the relevant social facts. By contrast, understanding law in explicitly normative terms has at least two important advantages. First, as Finnis notes, 'only [from] such a viewpoint is it a matter of overriding importance that law as distinct from other forms of social order should come into being, and thus become an object of the theorist's description'.[25] Conceptualising law as something practically important – that is, as the social instantiation of legality – focuses our enquiry upon normative orders that have a genuine impact upon the moral profiles of those they govern.[26] By necessity, this renders the study of law, and therefore of legal pluralism, a matter of normative

---

22 Dworkin (n 7) 201. The law-related beliefs of particular individuals matter for us at a later stage of analysis: see section 5 of this chapter and section 2 of chapter 3.

23 Habermas (n 21) 31.

24 For a discussion of Western ethnocentrism in legal pluralism, see chapter 1, section 6.

25 John Finnis, *Natural Law and Natural Rights* (OUP 1980) 15.

26 By 'moral profiles' we mean the complete sets of genuine practical reasons that apply to us, see: Mark Greenberg, 'The Moral Impact Theory of Law' (2014) 123(5) Yale LJ 1288, 1321–23.

importance. Under the 'plain fact' view of law or its more theoretically sophisticated positivist counterparts, the existence of a legal order *might* be normatively important. However, this is only ever a contingent matter.[27] Whether any number of texts, any collection of practices, or any convergence of official opinions genuinely matters will always depend upon the circumstances. Conversely, by focusing only upon those normative orders that, by virtue of their very essence, have an impact upon how people ought to behave, we guarantee that our enquiries will touch upon normatively salient issues.

Second, and for very similar reasons, our approach grapples with one important way in which legal orders can matter *to* those they govern. Engaged interpretation does more than merely observe what Hart refers to as 'the internal point of view': the perspective of those who believe that a given legal order provides genuine reasons for action.[28] It attempts, in a self-consciously external yet nonetheless invested manner, to reason *with* (even if not 'from within') that perspective.[29] As such, it brings non–culturally embedded social scientists as close as they can reasonably hope to be to accessing the *self*-understanding of a putative legal order. This is particularly important when engaging with a concept such as legal pluralism, given that many of the normative orders that exist in circumstances of legal plurality are non-hegemonic. As we shall see in Chapter 3, these include the legal orders of Indigenous peoples within settler-states and those of non-state peoples within postcolonial settings. Approaching such orders on the basis that they are normatively salient is one important way in which their often-embattled legal traditions can be shown respect by 'outsiders'.

3. What Legality Requires

We have characterised legality as a distinct mode of association through which communities instantiate civic equality by subjecting themselves to a single set of governing customs, principles, or rules. However, as Dworkin notes, such abstract characterisations remain 'almost entirely uninformative' without further specification of what the Rule of Law actually requires.[30] In this section, we provide a more definite account while still maintaining an understanding capacious enough to admit the many different forms and structures that contemporary legal orders take.

---

27 Cf. Hans Kelsen, *Essays in Legal and Moral Philosophy* (Ota Weinberger ed, Peter Heath tr, Springer 1973) 34.
28 HLA Hart, *The Concept of Law* (OUP 1994) 88–91.
29 Habermas (n 21) 26–27. For a counter perspective, see generally: Günter Frankenberg, *Comparative Law as Critique* (Edward Elgar 2016).
30 Ronald Dworkin, *Justice in Robes* (Harvard UP 2006) 169.

The Value(s) of Law and the Possibility of Its Plurality   43

Ultimately, the instantiation of legality must be identified in context, with abstract formulations getting one only so far. Indeed, any temptation to delimit legality *exclusively* in the abstract should be resisted. Doing so has tempted some theorists to assume that certain Western institutional forms are universal requirements for the presence of a legal order: an impulse we strongly resist.[31] Nonetheless, a modest and self-conscious resort to 'pure' philosophical reflection can be illuminating. It provides, as we shall see, an informative framework for the more concrete exercise of engaged interpretation.

As we have argued at some length elsewhere, legality has both horizontal and vertical dimensions.[32] These correspond, respectively, to relationships that exist (1) between and amongst individuals as private legal subjects and (2) between those subjects, taken as a set, and whatever governmental officials or traditional leaders might exist within the relevant order. Horizontally, legality secures civic equality by requiring each legal subject to behave with 'fidelity': an attitude of respect for the normative order that defines their community as a community of laws.[33] In this manner, each such community defines itself, at least in part, in terms of its members' mutual and reciprocal adherence to a shared set of governing standards. Such communities have, to borrow from Arendt, 'produced equality by organisation'[34] and may (all other things being equal) require compliance with their laws to the extent that observing and respecting such equality demands conformity.

By contrast, the vertical dimension of legality requires that 'force not be used or withheld, no matter how useful that would be to ends in view, no matter how beneficial or noble those ends, except as licensed and required by . . . past political decisions about when collective force is justified'.[35] In this respect, it limits arbitrary governmental power, forbidding fully discretionary decision-making by those in power.[36] What makes for effective limitations of this sort will naturally depend upon the size, form, and structure of the society over which power is being exercised. However, there is much to be said, at the abstract level, for examining normative orders in accordance with Fuller's eight desiderata

---

31 See, for example: Hart (n 28) 91–92.

32 Alex Green and Jennifer Hendry, 'Non-Positivist Legal Pluralism and Crises of Legitimacy in Settler States' (2019) 14(2) Journal of Comparative Law 267, 275–77; Alex Green and Jennifer Hendry, '*Ad Hominem* Criminalisation and the Rule of Law: The Egalitarian Case Against Knife Crime Prevention Orders' (2022) 42(2) OJLS 634, 636–40.

33 Lon Fuller, 'Postivism and Fidelity to Law – A Reply to Professor Hart' (1957) 71 Harvard LR 630.

34 Hannah Arendt, *The Origins of Totalitarianism* (Meridian Books 1958) 301.

35 Dworkin (n 7) 93.

36 Joseph Raz, *The Authority of Law: Essays on Law and Morality* (OUP 1979) 219–20.

of legality. These identify vertical legality with governance through customs, principles, or rules that are: (1) sufficiently general; (2) publicly promulgated; (3) prospective; (4) sufficiently intelligible; (5) non-contradictory; (6) relatively constant; (7) possible to obey; and (8) administered consistently with their apparent meaning.[37] Some normative orders can no doubt instantiate vertical legality without adhering to all eight desiderata. Fuller himself observes that where laws reflect the content of conventionally accepted morality, it is less important, even *vis-à-vis* legality, for them to be publicly promulgated and immediately intelligible.[38] For this reason, the Fullerian approach is sufficiently capacious to admit a broad range of culturally divergent instantiations of vertical legality.

Given the functional distinction between promoting civic equality and limiting arbitrary power, it may be difficult to see precisely what connects vertical legality with its horizontal counterpart or even why such connections matter. We argue that the unity of these two dimensions is secured in two ways, each of which turns upon a distinct political value to which legality is tied. The first such connection centers upon civic equality itself and the second upon individual autonomy. Insofar as they connect the two dimensions of legality, equality and autonomy fulfil the role of constitutive values, which not only explain legality's normative importance but also metaphysically ground the Rule of Law. Grounding, in this sense, means that the presence or absence of legality turns on the fact that those two more basic values are instantiated and promoted in social reality by a normative order that, by virtue of this very fact, can be said to take legal form.[39] The following two subsections outline these constitutive values and explain the role that both play in distinguishing the Rule of Law from other modes of governance. Having done so, the remainder of this section considers the concept of political legitimacy, arguing that legality's conceptual connections to equality and individual autonomy link it to promotion of legitimate governance in a very particular manner.

3.1 Civic Equality

On the account developed here, civic equality is central to the horizontal dimension of the Rule of Law. Although legal orders provide many different social advantages, such as mitigating coordination problems and

---

37 Fuller (n 5) 46–91.

38 ibid 92.

39 For more on the concept of metaphysical grounding, see: Ricki Bliss and Trogdon Kelly, 'Metaphysical Grounding' in Edward Zalta (ed), *The Stanford Encyclopaedia of Philosophy* (Winter edn, 2016) <https://plato.stanford.edu/archives/win2016/entries/grounding/>.

maintaining civil peace,[40] at their core lies the use of general standards as a means for instantiating the equal status of legal subjects.[41] Rousseau, for example, argued that laws properly so called must address the public as a whole rather than particular individuals or subgroups.[42] On this view, any purported law that is insufficiently general cannot be said to govern a community of collectively sovereign equals.[43] Although such considerations hold primarily in relation to legality's horizontal dimension, we can also identify them in the restrictions they place upon government. As Dworkin suggests, the *sine qua non* of vertical legality lies in a government's obligation to treat its subjects as equals, such that their interests are treated as being of equal importance.[44] This helps explain the normative significance of several of Fuller's eight desiderata. For example, on the reasonable assumption that equality of concern implies more-or-less consistent treatment, laws must be general in scope and administered consistently. Only then will each legal subject be treated as the civic equal of those with whom they share their community. Moreover, only when laws are both prospective and relatively constant will an individual be treated by those in power as the civic equal of their forebears and descendants. Indeed, as we argue elsewhere, one of the gravest Rule of Law violations that a government can commit is to undermine the egalitarian basis upon which legality rests.[45] Such violations are 'vertical' in that they are perpetrated by a government against its people but 'horizontal' in that they wrong individuals by undermining the bonds of civic equality they share.

3.2 Individual Autonomy

This relates to the capacity humans characteristically possess to make decisions for themselves, including long-term plans. Traditional liberal understandings of legality place considerable emphasis upon this capacity, arguing that the Rule of Law is geared primarily towards protecting

---

40 Immanuel Kant, *The Metaphysics of Morals* (Mary Gregor tr, CUP 2017) 49 [6:255–57]; Thomas Hobbes, *Leviathan* (JCA Gaskin ed, OUP 1996) 122.

41 TRS Allan, *Constitutional Justice: A Liberal Theory of the Rule of Law* (OUP 2001) 38–40.

42 Jean-Jacques Rousseau, 'On the Social Contract, or Principles of Political Right' in Donald Cress (tr), *The Basic Political Writings* (Hackett 1987) 150: 'For since the sovereign is formed entirely from the private individuals who make it up, it neither has nor could have an interest contrary to theirs'.

43 RA Duff, 'Inclusion and Exclusion: Citizen, Subjects and Outlaws' (1998) 51(1) Current Legal Problems 241, 253–56.

44 Dworkin (n 7) 222, 296.

45 Green and Hendry (n 32b) 642–51.

individual autonomy from arbitrary governmental action. Raz, for example, contends that:

> [V]iolation of the rule of law can take two forms. It may lead to uncertainty or it may lead to frustrated and disappointed expectations. It leads to the first when the law does not enable people to foresee future developments or to form definite expectations (as in cases of vagueness and most cases of wide discretion). It leads to frustrated expectations when the appearance of stability and certainty which encourages people to rely and plan on the basis of the existing law is shattered by retroactive law-making or by preventing proper law-enforcement, etc. The evils of uncertainty are in providing opportunities for arbitrary power and restricting people's ability to plan for their future.[46]

In a similar vein, Waldron emphasises the value of 'governance by general norms in a way that respects people's dignity as agents capable of autonomous self-government' as the essence of the Rule of Law.[47]

Although we share these liberal commitments, we worry that their almost exclusive focus upon legality's vertical dimension (exemplified by their recurrent emphasis upon *governance*) risks neglecting the connection between individual autonomy and the horizontal dimension of the Rule of Law. Communities of law are characterised, at least in part, by the publicly promulgated principles they provide for their members, around which those individuals can coordinate their behaviour. To use two paradigmatic Western legal examples, principles of contract increase individual autonomy by enhancing the reliability of commercial interaction amongst strangers,[48] while property laws allow private individuals to make complex plans in relation to their extant resources.[49] Such examples are indicative but by no means exclusive: any public standard that sufficiently instantiates Fuller's eight desiderata of legality will enable a community to organise their individual and collective lives around whatever obligations that standard entails. This matters because threats to individual autonomy come not only from arbitrary governmental power but also from inconsistent and overlapping private behaviour. Take the example of property laws. Living in constant apprehension of losing whatever we have accrued severely limits our ability to act autonomously. You and I cannot both make exclusive use of the same book at the same time or consume and enjoy all of the same drink. If we

46 Raz (n 36) 222.
47 Waldron (n 14) 1, 40–41.
48 Kant (n 40) 62, 65.
49 ibid 54–55, 89–90.

The Value(s) of Law and the Possibility of Its Plurality   47

try, at least one of our conflicting attempts will be frustrated. This injects uncertainty into our plans because, absent some form of coordination, there is a persistent risk of somebody acting incompatibly with us. A system of property rights alleviates this difficulty by providing a way to determine who has priority to a particular resource at any given time.

3.3 Political Legitimacy

As the previous subsections demonstrate, autonomy and equality help explain the normative importance of the Rule of Law in both its horizontal and vertical dimensions. In this way, they connect those two dimensions by showing them to be concerned with the same foundational values. We turn now from these values to another important political concept, which grounds legality in a somewhat different manner: by capturing a state of affairs that it is necessarily concerned with promoting. This concept is political legitimacy, which we define here as a state of affairs in which the exercise of governance is fully justified.[50] Broadly stated, governance is the process through which a community organises their collective lives and only requires justification when it becomes problematic in normative terms. This need for justification generally occurs due to the imposition of social and political hierarchies in combination with the use of collective social pressure or force as a means of coercion. To quote our previous characterisation of the issue:

> . . . [political *illegitimacy*] is [best] understood in terms of equality and autonomy: the elevation of *some* individuals (but not others) to positions of power presumptively violates equality, whilst coercion, understood as the exploitation of our capacity to reason by changing the options available to us, presumptively violates *both* equality and autonomy. This dual violation occurs because coercion subjugates the will of one person to that of another, which undermines their equal status and, through manipulation, also causes changes in behaviour, thus compromising autonomous decision-making.[51] [citations omitted]

From this perspective, it is clear that legality and legitimacy are closely linked, in that the values threatened by normatively problematic

---

50 Other work we have undertaken contains a somewhat more nuanced approach (for example: Alex Green, *Statehood as Political Community: International Law and the Emergence of New States* (CUP 2024) 170–78). As with the other normative concepts in this book, our approach to political legitimacy is explicitly functional, being tailored towards the elucidation of legal pluralism.

51 Green and Hendry (32a) 268.

governance (autonomy and equality) are the very same ones that ground the Rule of Law. Legality, in this sense, is not only a valuable mode of association but also a regulatory technique through which the risk of political illegitimacy can be lessened, at least to some degree. In abstract terms, the Rule of Law's overall conceptual position can be stated as follows: since legality is constituted by the promotion of autonomy and equality, its purpose can be at least partly understood in terms of its capacity to ameliorate governmental illegitimacy.

That this promotion of political legitimacy constitutes a *purpose* rather than just an important consequence of the Rule of Law is evident from legality's vertical dimension. The Rule of Law can be used to promote various beneficial social ends, such as the stabilisation of commerce and the consequent increase of domestic and international trade.[52] However, such benefits are only contingent consequences of legality as a regulatory technique rather than a necessary part of its normative structure. The vertical dimension of legality, concerned as it is with ensuring that governments respect the civic equality and autonomy of their subjects, is necessarily concerned with the promotion of political legitimacy.[53] When they become a function of administering publicly identifiable customs, principles, or rules, political hierarchies and even coercion can reinforce the equal treatment of legal subjects, which at least partly negates their presumptive violation of civic equality.[54] Moreover, insofar as such standards help to avoid coordination problems[55] and are sufficiently easy to identify by those subject to governance,[56] they can also enhance individual autonomy, consequently mitigating any violation of that value which may arise from their administration through coercive or hierarchical means. Lawmakers who promulgate governance standards, adjudicators who apply them, and those individuals who enforce them, may create 'equality and autonomy problems' insofar as their activity elevates them above their compatriots, who are subject to their rule.[57] However, to the extent that the normative orders such individuals work within instantiate legality, their activity also ameliorates those problems. Legality, as it were, partially 'dissolves' the problematic

---

52 See generally: Friedrich Hayek, *The Road to Serfdom* (Routledge 1944).

53 This also serves to distinguish the connection between legality and legitimacy from the equally important connection between legality and self-determination (see Section 6). Although legality promotes both of these values, legitimacy is something at which law necessarily *aims*, whereas self-determination is something that it *produces*. Although it is possible to conceive of collective self-determination without law, it is difficult to imagine legitimate governance in the absence of a legal order.

54 Dworkin (n 7) 213–14.

55 Kant (n 40) 27–29, 92–94, 97–98.

56 Fuller (n 5) 33–94.

57 Green (n 50).

nature of governance. For that reason, it is plausible to consider the Rule of Law as characteristically necessary for political legitimacy, even if it will not be sufficient in the vast majority of circumstances.[58]

4. The Problem of Plural Legality

The previous section explained our account of legality as a distinct set of political values by linking it to the connected concepts of civic equality, individual autonomy, and political legitimacy. In so doing, we expanded upon our earlier characterisation of the Rule of Law as a distinct mode of association through which a community becomes united under a single set of overarching customs, principles, or rules. In this section, we outline a philosophical puzzle that our approach to legality creates. This puzzle, which we refer to as 'the problem of plural legality', presents as follows. If the Rule of Law is grounded in the values of autonomy and equality because it promotes them through imposing *just one set* of coordinating standards, then how can any society be legally *plural*? The very notion of multiple normative orders, each having the status of law within the same social space, seems wholly antithetical to the account of legality provided previously. Nonetheless, the existence of legal pluralism appears, in some contexts, almost self-evident. How can this apparent paradox be explained?

Some scholars merely accept the concept of legal pluralism to be flatly inconsistent with thoroughgoingly normative accounts of law along the lines of the one provided earlier. This acceptance has tended to push them one of two ways. The first takes the problem of plural legality to imply that approaches to law of the sort we advance must be theoretically flawed. Legal pluralism, they claim, is a matter of social fact, and any theory that does not fit the relevant facts must, for that reason, be mistaken.[59] For example, Barber suggests that the problem of plural legality may require understandings of law like ours to overlook or define away the 'real-world contradictions identified by the pluralists',[60] which sits uneasily alongside the truism that '[t]here is no reason why such conflicts cannot arise and persist within and between legal institutions, even if we decline to accommodate or reflect on such disputes within legal philosophy'.[61]

---

58 Christopher Morris, *An Essay on the Modern State* (CUP 1998) 104.
59 William Twinning, 'A Symposium on Global Law, Legal Pluralism and Legal Indicators' 47(1) Journal of Legal Pluralism & Unofficial Law (2015) 1: 7.
60 Nick Barber, 'Legal Realism, Pluralism, and Their Challengers' in Ulla Neergaard and Ruth Nielsen (eds), *European Legal Method – Towards a New European Legal Realism* (DJØF Publishing 2013) 205.
61 ibid.

The second common approach to the problem of plural legality takes the opposite view. It posits that since a thoroughgoingly normative approach to the existence of law is not only possible but *necessary*, the apparent existence of legal pluralism must be an illusion. On this approach, what appears to be more than one legal order occupying the same social space is actually some other phenomenon, which requires explanation in different terms. In support of this conclusion, Letsas in particular offers two arguments. The first is definitional, addressing the commonplace pluralist distinction between state law and non-state law. His response to the objection that some legal philosophers wrongly synonymise 'law' with 'state-promulgated law' is that such objections are merely semantic, given that '[m]ost analytic legal philosophers use the words "legal system" to refer to a subcategory of normative systems, in which state institutions and officials play an important role'.[62] The pluralist challenge would only be significant, he claims, if it

> can embarrass legal philosophers about the way the latter identify that of which they do seek to give an account, namely *state*-ordained normative practices . . . If legal pluralism can show that there is either more state-ordained law (over-inclusive) or less state-ordained law (under-inclusive) than philosophical theories about the nature of law allow, then legal philosophers would have to modify their theories [emphasis in original].[63]

In addition to this definitional claim, Letsas advances a more contextual argument about constitutional pluralism within the European Union, which he describes as the 'legal philosopher's black swan' and so representative of the problem of plural legality in general.[64] Pointing to apparent conflicts between the norms of European Union law and those of Member States, Letsas claims that, at least characteristically, 'the requirements of the value of legality will be non-contradictory because the recalcitrant provisions that appear to generate conflict (wherever they may be found) will either be irrelevant, devoid of moral weight, or inconclusive. Law, on the non-positivist account, will turn out to be essentially *harmonic*'.[65] In particular, he claims that because 'non-positivism never infers that the demands of law are contradictory from the mere existence of conflicting rules or claims and the absence

---

62 George Letsas, 'Harmonic Law' in Julie Dickson and Pavlos Eleftheriadis (eds), *Philosophical Foundations of European Union Law* (OUP 2012) 77, 81.
63 ibid.
64 ibid.
65 ibid 99.

of any rules ranking them',[66] it is a mistake 'to ask who, the ECJ or national courts, has the ultimate authority to determine the competence of the EU (kompetenz-kompetenz)'.[67] Instead:

> [N]obody is to decide what falls within the competence of the EU because this question is objectively determined by moral facts to do with principles of social cooperation. Courts have to try to get these moral facts right, by taking EU norms as relevant only when this is justified by moral principles that apply to the scheme of cooperation in play . . . it is right that the efficacy of the joint scheme of co-operation, and the public goods it produces for its members, is jeopardized if different courts assign different boundaries to the domain of cooperation. But that is only an argument for courts to follow the same boundaries, not an argument that only one court (the ECJ or the national constitutional court) should have ultimate authority to set them.[68]

On this basis, according to Letsas, the task of the engaged interpreter should always be to resolve any seeming normative conflicts by focusing on what legal rights and duties exist within a particular social space, all things considered.[69] The question of whether more than one distinct legal order exists within that space is, on his view, otiose.

We find both approaches unsatisfying. The first, exemplified by Barber and Twining, risks begging the question. Legal pluralism might be self-evident in many circumstances, but self-evidence does not always imply social facticity. True, there are many self-evident social facts. In Yorkshire, where we both live, it is obvious to even the most casual observer that 'queue-jumping' is met with general disapproval and often with social censure. However, there are also many wholly uncontroversial normative facts: who could reasonably doubt that torturing people is wrong or that callous homicide is unjustifiable? Returning to legal pluralism, it cannot reasonably be doubted, for instance, that Suquamish law operates alongside United States law (both Federal and Washington State) within the Central Puget Sound Region. But this fact alone cannot prove that the existence of each discrete legal order and the legal pluralism which their overlapping claims create must therefore be questions of social fact alone. Eliding the existence of legal pluralism with its alleged social facticity in this way begs the question because it fails to engage even with the possibility that the problem of plural legality might have a normative solution. The interesting question, to put this point another way, is not

---

66 ibid 97.
67 ibid 100.
68 ibid.
69 ibid 97.

52   The Value(s) of Law and the Possibility of Its Plurality

whether legal pluralism pertains within areas such as the Central Puget Sound Region but *why* it does (and how we can come to know that this is so). Moral and political approaches, such as our own, do not accept the straightforward social facticity of *any* legal phenomenon, so they cannot be rejected by mere assertions that legal pluralism itself constitutes a social fact.

The second approach, advanced by Letsas, makes errors of a different sort. His definitional argument – that legal philosophers characteristically use 'law' to mean 'state-promulgated law' and that any disagreement with such usage is merely semantic – fails on two counts. First, it is empirically incorrect that legal philosophers as a set use the word 'law' in this way unless one possesses an artificially restricted view of what constitutes a legal philosopher (see Chapter 1). Second, even if this were not the case, by attempting to reduce the problem of plural legality to semantics, Letsas fundamentally misrepresents its normative importance. As we argue in some detail in what follows, the problem of plural legality matters because it is often crucial that non-state legal orders are recognised by 'outsiders' to instantiate the Rule of Law. Given the premise that both we and Letsas apparently share (that the existence of law denotes the presence of something worthy of a certain respect), refusing to acknowledge 'non-state law' solely to maintain definitional elegance is necessarily disrespectful. Moreover, when the non-state legal orders in question belong to Indigenous peoples who have been subjected to sustained colonial oppression, such terminological intransigence risks compounding imperialist discourses of 'primitiveness' and invalidity.

Finally, Letsas's contextual argument – that the appearance of constitutional pluralism within the European Union belies the reality of legal harmonisation – fares very poorly as a test case for the problem of legal plurality in general. The European Union is, in many senses, *sui generic*. As a supranational entity, it is categorically distinct from legal orders that exist within states, particularly those of Indigenous communities, which are characteristically subject to threats of 'incorporation' by the hegemonic legal order(s) of the state itself. It might not matter, *vis-à-vis* the European Union, which institutions get to pronounce upon the content and implications of its law. To those subject to unjust state hegemony, however, the power to give voice to an independent legal order is often crucial. As we argue in Section 6, for such substate groups, legality expresses not only the importance of negative, individual freedom but also the positive and collective freedom to self-determine as a community of laws and to assert an enduring identity, through the maintenance of a distinct legal tradition, against hegemonic forces.[70]

---

70   For more on this distinction, see: Isaiah Berlin, *Liberty* (2nd edn, OUP 2002) 1–54.

5. The Conditions for Legal Pluralism

The problem of plural legality presents a philosophical challenge for our account of law, but for the reasons just discussed, it is a challenge to be met head on rather than minimised or avoided. We need a framework for analysing legal pluralism that not only explains how its existence is consistent with the understanding of legality we adopt but also why approaching overlapping legal orders in this way is normatively important. Moreover, like any social-scientific framework, our characterisation of legal pluralism must not only 'fit' a sufficient number of paradigmatic cases to have explanatory power but must also enable us to distinguish between genuine cases of legal pluralism and merely apparent ones.

With this in mind, we take the conditions necessary for legal pluralism to be as follows. First, a provisionally identifiable community of people must be governed by two or more seemingly distinct sets of governance practices. Second, each such set of practices must ground at least some 'jural instances' (rights, duties, powers, liabilities, and so on),[71] which themselves are *prima facie* normatively binding for reasons of legality. Third, there must be a belief on the part of at least some relevant individuals that these sets of governance practices are in conflict, which is often most readily identifiable through the presence of ostensible conflicts between particular jural instances. Fourth, there must be no institution – no court, legislature, council, or similar – with both the capacity and political legitimacy to pronounce authoritatively upon these apparent conflict(s). These four conditions, which also provide our four stages for the identification of legal pluralism, are best explained in context and through example. That is the work of Chapter 3. Nonetheless, some more-or-less abstract characterisation can be usefully undertaken at this stage.

The first two conditions establish the existence of more than one *prima facie* legal order, represented by at least two governance traditions that instantiate legality. The second two conditions have a different function, being necessary to confirm their genuine separateness. Given the problem of plural legality, both the purpose and the constitutive values of the Rule of Law will ordinarily favour just one legal order existing in relation to any given community. As a matter of normative principle, therefore, establishing legal pluralism requires demonstrating that the relevant values would be better served by more than one order existing, notwithstanding this default position. This can be done, or so we argue, only by identifying apparent normative conflicts that are practically indefeasible at the institutional level without effecting some kind of injustice. In this respect, the

---

71 Hohfeldians call these 'jural instances', and hold them to exist in correlative pairs of 'jural relations', which is the language we adopt moving forward, see: Wesley Newcomb Hohfeld, 'Some Fundamental Legal Conceptions as Applied in Judicial Reasoning' (1913) 23 Yale LJ 16, 29–59.

relationship between legality and political legitimacy is crucial. As argued earlier, in its vertical dimension, the Rule of Law is in large part concerned with the promotion of legitimate governance. It follows from this that wherever the elimination or denial of plural legality would result in a loss of political legitimacy, there are strong normative reasons *of legality* for that plurality to be recognised and maintained, at least until a fully legitimate process for addressing it can be adopted. In practical terms, this means that no existing institution should attempt to resolve the apparent conflict between the relevant legal orders by 'incorporating' one into the other or by 'dissolving' both, so that a new order may arise. Under some circumstances, it will be suitable for an institution with *de facto* authority (that is, actual political power) to permit the non-hegemonic order to 'trump' its hegemonic competitor. Regrettably, this solution is rarely if ever opted for in practice. Chapter 3 considers several cases like this, focusing on those which arise in postcolonial and settler-state contexts, where legitimacy requires the maintenance and protection of Indigenous legal orders. In methodological terms, and as a consequence of this practical point, scholars must resist any urge either to unify or to 'harmonise' (as Letsas euphemistically puts it) pluralism out of existence. Whilst it might be aesthetically tempting to reconstruct the relevant conflicts so as to 'resolve' them, this must never be undertaken at the expense of engaging with the difficult and contextually embedded questions of political legitimacy that characteristically arise whenever legal pluralism truly pertains.

By understanding legal pluralism in terms of political legitimacy, our approach accomplishes something that is both pressing and distinct. Much like our understanding of law, it focuses attention on a conception of legal plurality that is necessarily important in normative terms. Illegitimate governance is a form of institutional injustice, where the rulers stand in a normatively inappropriate relationship to the ruled. As such, if legal pluralism pertains only where legitimacy itself mandates that more than one distinct legal order should be maintained, then it necessarily follows that legal plurality must be approached with care and respect. Conversely, where plural legality is under threat from hegemonic institutions or denied by those hell-bent on 'neatness' and uniformity, our approach readily supplies at least one reason such influences must be resisted.

6. Legal Pluralism and Self-Determination

As the foregoing discussion suggests, the account of legal pluralism with which we are now concerned both most commonly arises and is particularly important within societies in which two or more peoples stand in starkly asymmetric power relations. To appreciate the full implications of this, it is important to address one last value with which legality is intimately connected: that of collective self-determination. To see how this value connects with the importance of recognising and respecting legal pluralism, we must return to the problem of plural legality, which arises from the fact that legality is grounded in the values of autonomy and equality because it promotes political legitimacy by imposing a single set of coordinating standards upon communities that are governed by law. As we argued, there are nonetheless circumstances in which these constitutive values are better served by accepting the paradox of two or more coexisting legal orders rather than attempting to 'solve' it by 'incorporating' one order into the other. These circumstances arise when apparent conflicts between these orders cannot be addressed in a legitimate manner. From the perspective of legality, this lack of legitimacy matters because any attempts at governing by law that seriously undermine political legitimacy necessarily find themselves locked in conceptual and normative self-contradiction. However, from the perspective of self-determination, there can be even more at stake. Where political legitimacy is absent, the subordination of one legal order to another will also violate the moral right to self-determination enjoyed by the people to which the subordinated legal order attaches. This holds because where the maintenance of a distinct legal order is bound up with a people's exercise of self-determination, any unjustified acts of governmental domination directed against that order are necessarily also directed against the relevant people. Such domination becomes particularly problematic where the hegemonic order is used not only to subordinate but also to eliminate or replace the subject order: in such cases, the potential violation of self-determination is egregious.

Groups of individuals collectively self-determine when they live as 'peoples', which is to say as collectives that publicly manifest agency in the determining of their own fates.[72] Agency of this kind supervenes upon a certain degree of individual liberty, since the power that groups have to act is contingent upon the capacities of their members.[73] However, the self-determination of peoples is distinct from the exercise of personal freedom for two reasons. First, unlike individuals, groups possess neither 'inner lives' nor a sense of their own identity that cannot be reduced to the overlapping and often contested self-understandings that their individual

---

72 See, for example, discussion of that concept in: Christopher Wellman, *A Theory of Secession: The Case for Political Self-Determination* (CUP 2005); Omar Dahbour, *Self-Determination without Nationalism: A Theory of Postnational Sovereignty* (Temple UP 2012); Allen Buchanan, *Justice, Legitimacy, and Self-Determination: Moral Foundations for International Law* (OUP 2003).

73 Christian List and Philip Pettit, *Group Agency: The Possibility, Design, and Status of Corporate Agents* (OUP 2011) 19–41.

56 The Value(s) of Law and the Possibility of Its Plurality

members possess.[74] Second, while individuals characteristically pursue their own destinies within a social context over which they have little to no control, peoples often have considerable power to determine that context, which cannot be reduced to the power of any one member acting alone.[75] This second reason imbues collective self-determination with a particular kind of potency: that concerned with the creation of shared lifeworlds.[76] Whether this manifests as shared social norms, political institutions, economic arrangements, or spiritual traditions, groups exercising their power to self-determine each birth the worlds within which their individual members live, even though their capacity to do so is always conditioned by ecological, macroeconomic, and other inter- and trans-group background conditions.

At their largest and most formal, self-determining peoples constitute the populations of legally recognised states.[77] Indeed, self-determination itself provides an 'organising idea' for the international legal order, in terms of which many of its constitutive principles must be understood and applied.[78] Nonetheless, even within the relatively restrictive rubric of international law,[79] self-determination is recognised as both a value and right applicable to other peoples, including minorities, Indigenous peoples,[80]

---

74 Charles Beitz, *Political Theory and International Relations* (Princeton UP 1999) 75–76.
75 Seyla Benhabib, *Situating the Self: Gender, Community and Postmodernism in Contemporary Ethics* (Polity Press 1992) 23–38; Charles Taylor, *Philosophy and the Human Sciences: Philosophical Papers 2* (CUP 1985) 190.
76 Austin Harrington, 'Lifeworld' (2006) 23(1–3) Theory, Culture & Society 341.
77 UNGA Res 2625(XXV) (1974) UN Doc A/RES/2625(XXV), principle 5; Green (n 50) 72–75; James Crawford, *The Creation of States in International Law* (OUP 2007) 52–55; Antonio Cassese, *Self-Determination of Peoples: A Legal Reappraisal* (CUP 1995) 141–47.
78 Alex Green and Margaretha Wewerinke-Singh, 'State Continuity, Self-Determination, and Sea-Level Rise' (on file with authors). See also: International Covenant on Civil and Political Rights (ICCPR) (signed 16 December 1966, entered into force 23 March 1976) 999 UNTS 173, art 1; International Covenant on Economic, Social and Cultural Rights (ICESCR) (signed 16 December 1966, entered into force 3 January 1976) 993 UNTS 3, art 1; Committee on the Elimination of Racial Discrimination, *General Recommendation No. 21* (Forty-eighth session, 1996) UN Doc CERD/48/Misc.7/Rev.3, para 4 (1996); *Western Sahara (Advisory Opinion)* [1975] ICJ Rep p 12, para 5; Human Rights Committee (HRC), *ICCPR General Comment No. 12: Article 1 (Right to Self-Determination), The Right to Self-Determination of Peoples* (Twenty-first session, 1984) para 2; Stephen James Anaya, *Indigenous Peoples in International Law* (OUP 2004) 74.
79 Alex Green, 'Towards an Impossible Polis: Legal Imagination and State Continuity' in Alex Green, Mitchell Travis, and Kieran Tranter (eds), *Science Fiction as Legal Imaginary* (Routledge 2024).
80 United Nations Declaration on the Rights of Indigenous Peoples (UNDRIP), UNGA Res 61/295 (2007) UN Doc A/RES/61/295, arts 3–5; Sarah Joseph, Jenny Schultz, and Melissa Castan, *The International Covenant on Civil and Political Rights: Cases, Materials, and Commentary* (OUP 2005) 146.

The Value(s) of Law and the Possibility of Its Plurality   57

and the populations of non–self-governing and colonial territories.[81] The capacious nature of this concept – and in particular the fact that it applies to more than just recognised states – is borne out by sober reflection. The groups that bring value to our lives, be they civic, cultural, political, religious, or otherwise, cut across the states within which we find ourselves in various ways. Even nationality, which was historically linked to statehood,[82] in fact admits various multi- and plurinational arrangements within contemporary civic bodies.[83] Moreover, where several group identities overlap, such that a single people *not* in possession of statehood are nonetheless united by cultural, ethnic, religious, or substate political ties, it becomes even more morally important that the capacity of that people to self-determine is respected. This point helps explain why international law makes space for the possibility of 'internal' self-determination: the right of peoples within states to exercise agency over their own cultural, economic, political, and social destinies.[84] Whether international legal institutions are always successful in acknowledging and securing this right is something to which we return in Chapter 3.

One important means for the creation of the shared worlds through collective self-determination is the development of a distinctive legal order. As we argue previously, communities that instantiate legality tend towards having 'produced equality by organisation',[85] which alters their normative profile into that of a collective governed by laws. In so doing, their creation of a shared *nomos*, to borrow Cover's usage, generates 'a present world constituted by a system of tension between reality and vision', which 'build[s] relations between the normative and the material universe, between the constraints of reality and the demands of an ethic'.[86] This relationship between the communal creation of law by the practicing of it together and the development of a distinctive *nomos* means that, in any given case, 'at the bedrock of legality lie certain presuppositions on the part of participants concerning

---

81 ICCPR (n 78) art 1; ICESCR (n 78) art 1; Human Rights Committee, Consideration of Reports Submitted by States Parties under Article 40 of the Covenant (Fifty-first session, 1994) UN Doc CCPR/C/79/Add.38, para 6.

82 Christian Reus-Smit, *The Moral Purpose of the State: Culture, Social Identity, and Institutional Rationality in International Relations* (Princeton UP 2009) 87–121.

83 See generally: Michael Keating, *Plurinational Democracy: Stateless Nations in a Post-Sovereignty Era* (OUP 2001).

84 Cassese (n 77) 101–40; Richard Falk, 'The Rights of Peoples (In Particular Indigenous Peoples)' in James Crawford (ed), *The Rights of Peoples* (OUP 1988) 17–37; Garth Nettheim, ' "Peoples" and "Populations" – Indigenous Peoples and the Rights of Peoples' in ibid 107–26; Jennifer Hendry, 'A Legally Pluralist Approach to the *Bakassi Peninsula* Case' in Damian Gonzalez-Salzberg and Loveday Hodson (eds), *Research Methods for International Human Rights Law: Beyond the Traditional Paradigm* (Routledge 2020).

85 Hannah Arendt, *The Origins of Totalitarianism* (Meridian Books 1958) 301.

86 Robert Cover, 'Forward: Nomos and Narrative' (1983) 97 Harvard LR 4, 9.

58 The Value(s) of Law and the Possibility of Its Plurality

their ability in common to transform the world through their normative commitments'.[87] Understood thus, the twofold connection between law and self-determination is clear. On the one hand, peoples that govern themselves through law exhibit their collective agency through the creation and maintenance of a legal order which exists to govern *them*, as opposed to anyone else. On the other, through the augmentation of their shared normative universe, a people who self-determine through law do so by altering the normative background conditions in relation to which the day-to-day exercise of self-government takes place, thereby altering the reasons for behaviour which their community would otherwise possess.[88] Putting these two together, we can see that peoples who create for themselves a community of laws thereby self-determine *as* such a community: their relationship with legality, and in particular whatever distinctive form that relationship takes in cultural or institutional terms, becomes part of their collective identity as a people.

7. Conclusion

Much like law itself, legal pluralism is a contested concept (as we noted in the Introduction, it may even be essentially contested).[89] In the face of the deep and inescapable controversy that surrounds its meaning and application, this chapter cleaved to an understanding of law and

87 Emmanuel Melissaris, *Ubiquitous Law: Legal Theory and the Space for Legal Pluralism* (Ashgate Press 2009) 104–5.

88 According to both Cover and Melissaris (cited previously) these changes are intersubjective, in the sense that the reasons for action or obligations generated by the adoption of legal practices exist only relatively amongst the adopting group, insofar as they share an 'ethic' or particular 'presuppositions', to use phrases from those authors. Our view is different. We take the relevant changes in normative reasons to be 'real' or 'genuine', in the sense that they both exist and carry weight for those to whom they apply, no matter what anyone believes about them. (Beliefs matter, on our account, for different reasons; see Section 2 of Chapter 3.) Self-determination happens insofar as self-governance through law *successfully* alters what Greenberg calls the 'moral profile' of the people in question, see: Greenberg (n 26) 1306–11. To quote an example from Greenberg himself (ibid 1311), 'it is clear that agents who break at least some promises have resulting obligations to the promisee, but there is a great deal of uncertainty about what sorts of remedial actions are appropriate with respect to different promises, and it is plausible that there are frequently a variety of different ways in which the remedial obligations can be met. Once the legal system provides certain contract remedies, however, people who make promises act against that background, and this can render determinate and certain or otherwise change what is morally required in the event of breach'. [References omitted.] By altering the normative background conditions that apply to them in this manner, communities constituted by law function as self-determining peoples by developing a unique moral profile across time.

89 WB Gallie, 'Essentially Contested Concepts' (1955) 56 Proceedings of the Aristotelian Society 167.

its plurality that emphasises what we consider to be most normatively important and distinctive about both. We began by explaining what it means for law to exist as a particular set of normative considerations commonly referred to as 'the Rule of Law' or 'legality'. Next, we developed an abstract account of what legality requires, detailing its connection to the values of equality, individual autonomy, and political legitimacy. We then explained the challenge posed by 'the problem of plural legality': a philosophical conundrum which seems to suggest that the very concept of the Rule of Law is at odds with the existence of legal pluralism. We argued that this philosophical challenge can be solved by paying close attention to the relationship that exists between political legitimacy as a normatively important goal and legality as a regulatory technique that is necessarily dedicated to promoting that end. Finally, we detailed the connections between legality and collective self-determination, which provide another important reason for the emergence of legal pluralism to be recognised and respected.

In the course of this argument, we presented four conditions for the existence of legal pluralism. Our language on this point is worth replicating. First, a provisionally identifiable community of people must be governed by two or more seemingly distinct sets of governance practices. Second, each such set of practices must ground at least some jural instances, which are *prima facie* morally binding for reasons of legality. Third, there must be a belief on the part of at least some relevant individuals that these sets of governance practices are mutually incompatible. Fourth, there must be no institution – that is, no court, legislature, council, or similar – with both the capacity and political legitimacy to pronounce authoritatively upon these apparent conflict(s). The next chapter considers the application of these conditions within postcolonial and settler-state contexts.

Chapter 3

Colonial Injustice and Legal Pluralism

1. Introduction

Legal pluralism, we have argued, exists when four conditions are met. First, a provisionally identifiable community of people must be governed by two or more seemingly distinct sets of governance practices. Second, each such set of practices must ground at least some jural instances, which are *prima facie* binding upon that community for reasons of legality. Third, there must be a belief on the part of at least some relevant individuals that these sets of governance practices are mutually incompatible, which is often (but not always) demonstrated by showing that the jural instances they ground are treated as though they were in conflict. Fourth, there must be no institution – no court, legislature, council, or similar – with both the capacity and political legitimacy to authoritatively pronounce upon these apparent conflicts. In this chapter, we apply this framework to a range of circumstances within settler and postcolonial states, each of which meets all four conditions for legal pluralism. We begin with a general characterisation of why our conception of legal pluralism is apt to arise in jurisdictions with colonial legacies, which focuses upon the injustice of colonialism and its implications for both political legitimacy and collective self-determination. We then examine settler and postcolonial states in turn as discrete socio-legal categories, emphasising the cultural, political, and social complexities that exist within them and how those complexities give rise to legal pluralism.

2. Colonialism, Injustice, and Illegitimacy

As noted in Chapter 2, governance is morally problematic insofar as it violates autonomy and equality: illegitimacy pertains wherever governance employs social and political hierarchies or coercion that cannot be appropriately justified. Indeed, the importance of autonomy and equality sets the threshold for legitimacy quite high, such that the instantiation of legality alone will typically not be enough to prevent governmental

DOI: 10.4324/9781003532149-4

illegitimacy from occurring. At minimum, at least within contemporary states, the maintenance of civil peace, the protection of fundamental human rights, and appropriately representative government seem to be necessary in addition to the Rule of Law if the *prima facie* wrongfulness of governance is to be addressed. Through a combination of providing independent goods, like civil peace,[1] and by dissolving the problematic aspects of governance by making its exercise a function of both autonomy and equality,[2] this combination of features might even be *sufficient* to justify some governmental activity that would otherwise be morally impermissible. For example, where the maintenance of civil peace creates circumstances of greater justice than those of pervasive anarchy, it will be legitimate to impose political hierarchies and coercive practices necessary to guarantee that peace.[3]

However, abstract propositions like these lack the historical context necessary to make all-things-considered judgements about political legitimacy. In particular, histories of great injustice inevitably contour the moral profiles of contemporary societies, such that accounts of justice and legitimacy within those societies cannot take refuge in abstraction if they are to remain accurate. Within postcolonial and settler-states, where the normative profile of contemporary governance is influenced by the legacies of an imperial past, this is particularly clear. Indeed, we argue that the threshold for legitimacy is often extremely high within such states, where ongoing legacies of colonialism can intractably complicate or undermine the justifiability of state governance *vis-à-vis* Indigenous peoples and other minority groups.

The injustice of colonialism is fundamentally tied to its violation of autonomy, equality, and self-determination. In material terms, the 'full horror of the atrocities committed' by European imperial powers is difficult to calculate.[4] In many cases, the widespread murder of Indigenous peoples together with the non-recognition of their communities and the dismantling of their governance institutions clearly amounted to genocide.[5] There have also been several instances in which surviving peoples were enslaved, subject to forced migration, and substantially deprived of access to necessary resources.[6] However, in addition to these material

---

1 Alex Green, *Statehood as Political Community: International Law and the Emergence of New States* (CUP 2024) 182–83.

2 ibid.

3 Thomas Hobbes, *Leviathan* (Penguin Classics 1997) 122.

4 Bartolomé de las Casas, *A Short Account of the Destruction of the Indies* (Penguin Random House 1992) 43.

5 For example, see the visceral account of these trends within the Australian Aboriginal context by Irene Watson, *Aboriginal Peoples, Colonialism and International Law: Raw Law* (Routledge 2014) 67–144; 'Buried Alive' (2002) 13 Law and Critique 253.

6 For instance, the physical, biological, and cultural genocide found in: The Truth and Reconciliation Commission of Canada, *Honouring the Truth, Reconciling for the Future*

harms, colonialism as an ongoing process possesses the distinct and transactional wrongfulness 'of a form of association that fails to offer equal and reciprocal terms of interaction to all its members'.[7] By forcing and manipulating Indigenous peoples into subordinate positions, the European powers disrespected and undermined the autonomy and equal status of each individual within those communities.[8] Moreover, insofar as this process of subordination itself undermined self-governance by colonised peoples, it not only violated their moral entitlement to self-determination as such but also expressively disrespected their *capacity* to self-determine by creating an asymmetrical relationship at the collective level. As Green explains:

> [P]olitical action within the dominated communit[ies was] objectively disrespected [by colonial powers], simply by the fact that [their] population[s were] denied an institutional structure . . . primarily concerned with governing *them*, as opposed to any other population. Consider the British government's relationship with colonial India. During colonial rule, the former directly governed England, Wales, Scotland, and (at least to some extent) Ireland. Whilst almost certainly not legitimate in respect of those populations . . . the British government at least purported to exist for their benefit and/or primarily for the purpose of preventing endemic conflict amongst them. Individuals living within Britain thereby lived under institutions whose governance was nominally an end, rather than a means. Conversely, the British government did not even purport to govern India solely for the benefit of those who lived there: British nationals were considered to have a stake in colonial government as well.[9] [Emphasis in original; references omitted.]

The normative result of this (often ongoing) subordination is that the very same values intrinsic to legality – autonomy, equality, and legitimacy – are undermined by the establishment of new societies on colonial terms. In contemporary contexts, this creates discrete challenges when establishing political legitimacy for the purposes of addressing apparent conflicts between overlapping legal orders implicated by these colonial legacies.

Summary of the Final Report of the Truth and Reconciliation Commission of Canada (2015) <http://nctr.ca/assets/reports/Final%20Reports/Executive_Summary_English_Web. pdf> last accessed 23 January 2024.

7 Lea Ypi, 'What's Wrong with Colonialism' (2013) (41) Philosophy & Public Affairs 158, 178.

8 ibid 179–81.

9 Green (n 1) 91.

The governance institutions of settler-states, by virtue of their origins and ongoing complicity in the subordination of Indigenous peoples, are often fundamentally undermined in terms of their legitimacy *vis-à-vis* these groups. As such, it is far harder for such institutions to evince sufficient legitimacy to sidestep the fourth condition for legal pluralism we set out. This follows from a more general proposition concerning corrective justice: when a moral wrong is committed, the onus is upon the wrongdoer either to reverse the unjust state of affairs or to do the next-best thing by providing reparations.[10] Neither action can erase the original wrong; however, taking appropriate action can prevent that violation from becoming compounded. The enhanced legitimacy threshold in settler-states *vis-à-vis* Indigenous peoples reflects the importance of responding to considerations of this kind. Legitimate governance within such states requires more than *general* justifications relying, for example, on the provision of representative government or the instantiation of legality: it also requires *specific* justification in relation to the contemporary implications of its unjust past. In some circumstances, this requirement can be so thoroughgoing that any failure to address the ongoing injustices of colonial governance represents what we elsewhere call a 'legitimacy crisis'.[11] The result is that legal pluralism arises within settler-states almost by definition: it is in the nature of settler-colonialism that it (unjustly) imposes hegemonic normative orders upon the existing practices of Indigenous peoples and, in so doing, suppresses those practices, characteristically through violence.

The position in postcolonial states is different. Unlike settler-states, where hegemonic governance institutions are characteristically identical with their colonial forebears,[12] postcolonial institutions at least nominally represent peoples who were themselves once victims of colonial domination rather than those perpetrating or materially benefiting from that wrong.[13] As such, where state and non-state legal orders conflict within a postcolonial context, the situation is often one in which *all* the people(s) in question have shared histories of subordination to the same colonial powers. The legitimacy challenges that arise in these circumstances are typically tied up with the process of decolonisation itself,

---

10 Aristotle, *Nichomachean Ethics* (Sarah Broadie and Christopher Rowe trs, OUP 2002) 1130b30–1b20.
11 Alex Green and Jennifer Hendry, 'Non-Positivist Legal Pluralism and Crises of Legitimacy in Settler-States' (2019) 14(2) Journal of Comparative Law 267. See also: David Lyons, *Confronting Injustice: Moral History and Political Theory* (OUP 2013) 106.
12 Lyons (n 11).
13 This sense of 'representation' involves 'speaking for' a group, akin to 'acting in their place' (Hanna Pitkin, *The Concept of Representation* (University of California Press 1967) 82). Our point is not that such individuals actually *are* representative of those they govern (which might help to justify their activity) but that they *act as though they were* (ibid).

under which non–self-governing territories gained independence from their metropolitan states as complete units, notwithstanding the considerable cultural, ethnic, and religious differences that characterised their resident populations.[14] As a matter of international law, this was typically justified via appeal to the principle *uti possidetis juris*, which operated in the context of decolonisation to maintain extant territorial boundaries out of concern for regional peace and stability.[15] One important implication of this practice, managed as it was by the so-called 'Great Powers' under the auspices of the United Nations, was that many peoples were afforded the opportunity to self-determine only as part of a state, the borders and membership of which they had no real opportunity to help define.[16] Consequently, postcolonial state institutions often find themselves interacting with non-state legal orders attached to peoples in relation to whom they are asymmetrically placed, either because the groups in question constitute politically and socially marginalised minorities or because postcolonial institutions have adopted the colonial-era practice of subordinating the legal orders of such groups to their own. This leaves such institutions in a complex normative position: although their attachment to political communities with a shared history of subordination to one or more European powers entails that *externally*, their legitimacy is assured, the same does not always hold *internally* against peoples with claims to self-determination that are no less sound than those of the postcolonial states against which they are now often pitted. Insofar as the self-determination of these Indigenous and other non-state peoples is tied to the operation of one or more non-state legal orders, the legacy of colonialism once more creates space for legal pluralism.

Understood in this manner, the moral profiles of postcolonial and settler-states helps explain the salience of our third condition for legal pluralism: that some relevant individuals must *believe* in the conflicting nature of the legal orders in question. The problem of plural legality requires that only one set of governing principles apply to a given community unless the constitutive values of the Rule of Law would be better served by recognising and preserving the application of more than one legal order. When identifying such situations, the importance of law as a

---

14 Llyod Fallers, 'Customary Law in the New African States' (1962) 27(4) Law and Contemporary Problems 605.

15 Alex Green, 'Three Reconstructions of "Effectiveness": Some Implications for State Continuity and Sea-level Rise' (2024) 44(2) OJLS 201, 210–211; Steven Ratner, *The Thin Justice of International Law: A Moral Reckoning of the Law of Nations* (OUP 2015) 173–76.

16 Jennifer Hendry, 'A Legal Pluralist Approach to the *Bakassi Peninsula* Case' in Damian Gonzalez-Salzberg and Loveday Hodson (eds), *Research Methods for International Human Rights Law: Beyond the Traditional Paradigm* (Routledge 2019) 136–42.

means for collective self-determination must be kept in mind. Although scholars, insofar as they are 'engaged interpreters' along the lines of those detailed within Chapter 2, can attempt to ascertain the existence of conflict from an 'external yet invested' point of view, special precedence must be given to the perspectives of those either subject to or responsible for administering the legal orders involved. This holds for two reasons. First, due to a range of normative considerations, we must operate under the (albeit rebuttable) presumption that individuals embedded within a particular legal order are better placed to identify the normative implications of that order than those with no direct experience of its operation.[17] Second, a people's presumptive authority to interpret their own legal practices is an important aspect of their capacity to self-determine through law. This authority is rarely challenged in relation to the hegemonic legal orders of established states, where the findings of law-applying institutions provide paradigmatic 'raw data' for legal interpretation. Even in circumstances like those of the European Union, where Member States receive binding rulings from institutions outwith their own, the findings of domestic institutions in relation to their own legal orders are almost always treated with respect. Within the postcolonial or settler-state context, this does not always hold for non-state legal orders. As such, it becomes particularly important *vis-à-vis* self-determination for the law-related beliefs expressed by subjects and officials of these non-hegemonic legal orders to be treated as particularly probative by external observers. In what follows, we apply these insights to various examples within states of both kinds.

3. Legal Pluralism in Settler-States

The settler-states with which we are most immediately concerned are Canada, the Commonwealth of Australia, New Zealand (Aotearoa), and the United States of America, which are often grouped together under the acronym of 'CANZUS' states. Considering these jurisdictions collectively is instructive, not least because they are 'all affluent liberal democracies settled [through]. . . intensive British imperial expansion . . . and many of their current legal-constitutional commonalities

---

17 See generally: Mary Turpel, 'Aboriginal Peoples and the Canadian Charter: Interpretive Monopolies, Cultural Differences' (1990) 6 Canadian Human Rights Yearbook 3; Penelope Pether, 'Principles or Skeletons? Mabo and the Discursive Constitution of the Australian Nation' (1998) 41 Law Text Culture 115; Michael Cooke, *Indigenous Interpreting Issues for Courts* (The Australian Institute of Judicial Administration 2002); Jo-Anne Byrne, *The Perpetuation of Oral Evidence in Native Title Claims* (National Native Title Tribunal 2002).

66 Colonial Injustice and Legal Pluralism

derive from their shared inheritance of English common law'.[18] In addition to this historical pedigree, their institutional commonalities can be explained with reference to the fact that within hegemonic legal orders promulgated by political communities of their complexity, the constitutive values of legality demand particular kinds of governance practices. For example, the size of CANZUS states alone would seem to require a certain degree of centralised administration, as well as a process for legislation via the promulgation of publicly accessible legal texts, without which the progressive realisation of both autonomy and equality would suffer from significant coordination problems.[19]

So central do these institutional commonalities seem to legality within many contemporary Western states, CANZUS settler-states included, that they have often been mistaken for necessary features of law as such. For example, Waldron takes it as axiomatic that 'legal systems' cannot exist without the presence of courts, which he defines as:

> institutions that apply norms and directives established in the name of the whole society to individual cases, that settle disputes about the application of those norms, and that do so through the medium of hearings-formal events that are tightly structured to enable an impartial body to fairly and effectively determine the rights and responsibilities of particular persons after hearing evidence and argument from both sides.[20]

Clearly, this is far more particular than the idea of law-applying institutions or officials,[21] which admits bodies that, from a Western legal perspective, might be considered highly informal. Nonetheless, our account of legality does not entail that law exists only where such 'mode[s] of operation or procedure',[22] to use Waldron's phrase, pertain.[23] Like any other moral value, the application of legality must be sensitive to cultural, historical, and social context.[24] In the case of some Indigenous legal orders, the peoples governed by those orders are far smaller and more closely connected by cultural and spiritual ties than the sprawling and internally diverse populations of contemporary states. Given this context, it can sometimes be less important *vis-à-vis* both autonomy and equality for Indigenous legal orders to be administered in wholly

---

18 Kirsty Gover, 'Settler-State Political Theory, "CANZUS" and the UN Declaration on the Rights of Indigenous People' (2015) 26(2) EJIL 345, 356.

19 Lon Fuller, *The Morality of Law* (Yale UP 1977) 49–51.

20 Jeremy Waldron, 'The Concept and the Rule of Law' (2008) 43(1) Georgia LR 1, 20.

21 Joseph Raz, *Practical Reason and Norms* (Princeton UP 1990) 136–36.

22 Waldron (n 20) 22.

23 See also: Ronald Dworkin, *Justice in Robes* (Harvard UP 2008) 184.

24 Bernard Williams, *Ethics and the Limits of Philosophy* (Routledge 1985) 65–68.

impersonal terms,[25] along the lines of what Hart calls a 'modern munici-pal legal system'.[26] In this section, we examine some indicative encoun-ters between the legal orders of CANZUS settler-states and the diverse Indigenous legal orders that exist alongside them. Our aim in each case is not only to exemplify the account of legal pluralism developed so far but also to demonstrate why it is instructive to analyse such encounters in the normatively engaged manner we advocate.

3.1 An American Legitimacy Crisis: The Case of Mark Oliphant v. Suquamish Indian Tribe

Our first example is the 1978 United States Supreme Court case of *Oliphant*, which declared tribal governments to lack the authority to pros-ecute non-Indians who commit crimes within Indian Country.[27] Mark Oliphant, a non-Indian living on the Suquamish's Port Madison Indian Reservation during the summer of 1973, attended a tribal celebration at which he assaulted a tribal police officer and resisted arrest. After his arrest and charge by tribal police, Oliphant faced prosecution before the Provisional Court of the Suquamish Indian Tribe, which claimed author-ity to try non-Indians under the tribe's Law and Order Code,[28] 'by rea-son of their retained national sovereignty'.[29] Arguing that the Suquamish lacked jurisdiction over him as a non-Indian, Oliphant sought habeas cor-pus relief under the 1968 Indian Civil Rights Act (ICRA).[30] The question facing the Supreme Court was whether the Suquamish genuinely retained inherent criminal authority to prosecute non-Indians. In a controversial opinion, Justice Rehnquist found in favour of Oliphant, thereby reject-ing decades of precedent and diminishing the efficacy of tribal criminal jurisdiction with lasting effect.[31] In so doing, Rehnquist also reversed an earlier ruling in the same matter by the United States Federal Court of Appeals for the Ninth Circuit, which held that 'the power to preserve order on the reservation, when necessary by punishing those who vio-late tribal law, is a sine qua non of the sovereignty that the Suquamish

25 Fuller (n 19) 92.
26 HLA Hart, *The Concept of Law* (3rd edn, OUP 2012) 1–6, 91–109.
27 *Mark Oliphant v Suquamish Indian Tribe* 435 US 191 (1978). Indian Country, as defined by federal statute at 18 USC § 1151 (2012), includes all reservations, dependent Indian communities, and Indian allotments to which title has not been extinguished.
28 1973, ch 1, art I(d), §3.
29 *Oliphant* (n 27) 196.
30 25 US Code §§1301–4 at §1303.
31 For a full account of these effects, see: Sarah Krakoff, 'Mark the Plumber v Tribal Empire, or Non-Indian Anxiety v Tribal Sovereignty? The Story of *Oliphant v Suquam-ish Indian Tribe*' in Carole Goldberg, Kevin Washburn, and Philip Frickey (eds), *Indian Law Stories* (Foundation Press 2011).

68 Colonial Injustice and Legal Pluralism

originally possessed'.[32] By making this move, or so we argue here, the Supreme Court compounded the illegitimacy of the hegemonic institutions of United States of America (US) in relation to the Indigenous peoples that live within its borders.

Locating legality in the self-governance practices of the relevant Indigenous legal order is straightforward in *Oliphant*. Contrary to the now largely discredited doctrines of discovery and *terra nullius*, the territory of what is now the US was originally home to numerous peoples, many of which possessed distinctive legal orders.[33] Indeed, to quote Hendry and Tatum, '[t]ribal governments, like all other governments, have always possessed methods for settling disputes and dealing with those who violate community norms'.[34] Unlike 'the formal court system of the Europeans', these methods often included mediation by tribal elders,[35] and even today have regular and frequent recourse to customary law.[36] As noted previously, however, divergence from the Western legal paradigm in itself does not preclude the fundamentally legal nature of these practices. What matters is whether they instantiate the Rule of Law.

Taking their name from the traditional Lushootseed phrase for 'people of the clear salt water', the Suquamish and their ancestors inhabited the Central Puget Sound Region (in present-day Washington) for thousands of years. A federally recognised tribe, the Suquamish now live on the Port Madison Indian Reserve. As a party to the 1855 Treaty of Point Elliott, the sovereign Suquamish government relinquished title to their extant lands for acknowledgement and protection of their fishing and hunting rights, healthcare, education, and the reservation at Port Madison.[37] The tribe are currently governed according to their own Suquamish Tribal Code,[38] which codified the 1973 Law & Order Code, the Youth Code, and various other Tribal Council–published resolutions and ordinances. In 1978, when *Oliphant* was decided, the Suquamish possessed a Tribal Council, courts, police, and other institutions established by their constitution and bylaws (adopted 23 May 1965), through which they governed their

---

32 Quoted in the 9th circuit case *Mark David Oliphant v Edward Schlie, Chief of Police of the City of Bremerton, Defendant* 544 F.2d 1007 (9th Cir. 1976), 1009.

33 John Borrows, *Recovering Canada: The Resurgence of Indigenous Law* (Toronto UP 2002) 117.

34 Jennifer Hendry and Melissa Tatum, 'Justice for Native Nations: Insights from Legal Pluralism' (2018) 60 Arizona LR 91, 105.

35 Melissa Tatum, 'Civil Jurisdiction: The Boundaries between Federal and Tribal Courts' (1997) 29 Arizona State LJ 705, 708–9.

36 Matthew Fletcher, 'Rethinking Customary Law in Tribal Court Jurisprudence' (2007) 13 Michigan Journal of Race and Law 57, 60–61.

37 Treaty with the Dwamish, Suquamish, etc, 22 January 1885, Point Elliott, 12 Stat. 927.

38 Suquamish Tribal Council Resolutions: 88-048, 11 July 1988; 91–106, 28 October 1991.

Colonial Injustice and Legal Pluralism 69

collective lives.[39] Furthermore, although not lacking its own controversy,[40] ICRA required all 'Indian tribes' to implement many of the guarantees provided in the US Bill of Rights.[41]

These practices and institutions are patently sufficient to satisfy the horizontal dimension of legality by grounding governance standards that established the Suquamish tribe as a community of equals. Indeed, parallels might be drawn between the Suquamish legal order and the settler-state order of the US itself,[42] such that if we accept the legality of those hegemonic state practices, doubting the status of Suquamish law seems entirely unmotivated. This parallel also extends to legality's vertical dimension. If we believe that the governance practices found within US federal law 'commit [that community]. . . to the following political and legal ideals: government must treat all those subject to its dominion as having equal moral and political status',[43] consistency requires us to holds exactly the same for the Suquamish legal order. Oliphant himself, for example, was formally charged before the Provisional Court of the Suquamish Indian Tribe, incarcerated by order of that court, then released on his own recognisance. This process has all the hallmarks of legally regulated governmental coercion.

Understanding the significance of *Oliphant* requires three points of context. First, it is quite ordinary for non-Indians to be resident in Indian Country. At the time of the Supreme Court ruling, the 2,928 non-Indian residents of Port Madison Indian Reservation outnumbered the 50 Suquamish residents by a ratio of almost 60 to 1.[44] This asymmetry occurred due to the federal government's assimilationist allotment policy, whereby the 1887 General Allotment (Dawes) Act led to significant percentages of tribal land passing out of Indian hands.[45] Second, in its 'wholesale creation of a limiting theory of tribal jurisdiction', the

39 Robert Ruby and John Brown, *A Guide to the Indian Tribes of the Pacific Northwest* (revised edn, University of Oklahoma Press 1992) 228.
40 Milner Ball, 'Constitution, Court, Indian Tribes' (1987) 12(1) American Bar Foundation Research Journal 1, 123–24.
41 25 US Code §§ 1301–4.
42 On the shift to 'Western-style constitutional tribal government in 1934' and the move away from traditional procedures, see Russell Barsh and James Henderson, 'The Betrayal: Oliphant v Suquamish Indian Tribe and the Hunting of the Snark' (1979) 63 Minnesota LR 609, 636; and Hendry and Tatum (n 34) 104–10.
43 Ronald Dworkin, *Freedom's Law: The Moral Reading of the American Constitution* (Harvard UP 1996) 7–8.
44 *Oliphant* (n 27) 193(n.1). US Census data from 2020 shows that, even that recently, Indians and Alaskan Natives comprised only 13.9% of the Port Madison Reservation: <https://data.census.gov/table?g=2500000US2925_2800000US532925&d=DEC%20 Demographic%20Profile> last accessed 30 January 2024.
45 Codified as amended at 25 US Code §§ 331–34, 339, 341–42, 348–49, 354, 381 (2006). When delivering judgement, the Rehnquist Court itself noted that the 'substantial non-Indian population on the Port Madison Reservation is primarily the result of the

Supreme Court was plainly concerned about 'the specter [sic] of fifty reservation tribal members exercising criminal authority over nearly three thousand non-Indian reservation residents'.[46] This judicial discomfort with the regulation of non-Indians by tribal law is clear from the Court's reliance on the 1883 decision of *Ex Parte Crow Dog*, which it employed to argue against judging non-Indians

> by a standard made by others and not for them [and also against trying] them, not by their peers, nor by the customs of their people, nor the law of their land, but by a . . . different race, according to the law of a social state of which they have an imperfect conception.[47]

Rehnquist's approach on this point was particularly incongruous, given that Congress had explicitly taken steps, in the form of ICRA, to guarantee the rights of all defendants in tribal courts, whether Indian or non-Indian.[48] Third, to the considerable detriment of public safety, *Oliphant* created a prosecutorial lacuna within tribal criminal law enforcement. Considering the large number of non-Indians resident within the Port Madison Indian Reservation and, as Rehnquist himself noted, 'the prevalence of non-Indian crime on today's reservations',[49] this constituted a particularly egregious attack on the capacity of the Suquamish to maintain law and order. This created significant jurisdictional uncertainty within Indian Country across the US, which is problematic *vis-à-vis* legality in its own right. By compelling tribes to rely upon federal law enforcement, it also made them increasingly dependent upon 'another sovereign's law-enforcement interests',[50] thereby

---

    sale of Indian allotments to non-Indians by the Secretary of the Interior', see: *Oliphant* (n 27) 193(n.1).

46 N Bruce Duthu, 'Implicit Divestiture of Tribal Powers: Locating Legitimate Sources of Authority in Indian Country' (1994) 19(2) American Indian LR 353, 376.

47 *Oliphant* (n 27) 210–11, quoting *Ex Parte Crow Dog* 109 US 558 (1883) at 571. The great irony of this, perhaps, is that *Crow Dog* itself held that federal courts lacked criminal jurisdiction over Indians in Indian Country and was, in that limited respect, a precedent in favour of Indigenous self-determination. On a more concrete level, the use of *Crow Dog* in *Oliphant* is particularly insidious given that the motivation behind the former ruling was to protect an Indian from being held in violation of a criminal law that carried the death penalty when there was no notice that the law in question even applied to them in the first place. Mark Oliphant, by contrast, who drunkenly punched a Tribal law enforcement officer in the nose, had lived within the Port Madison Reservation voluntarily for some time. There can be no serious suggestion that criminal punishment, in those circumstances, would have been unexpected. (We are grateful to Melissa Tatum for putting this point to us in these terms.)

48 Barsh and Henderson (n 42) 635.

49 *Oliphant* (n 27) 212.

50 Judith Resnik, 'Multiple Sovereignties: Indian Tribes, States, and the Federal Government' (1995) 79(3) Judicature 118, 124.

suppressing their ability to self-govern through the institution of effective criminal law.[51]

It should be clear from the foregoing that the apparent conflict between the Suquamish and US federal law was profound. The principles comprising the Suquamish legal order grounded a power on the part of tribal officials to prosecute crimes within the Port Madison Reservation, to which both Indians and non-Indians were liable.[52] The irreconcilable claim of the Rehnquist Court alleged that non-Indians were immune from this tribal power of prosecution, which, if true, would have disabled the tribal court from trying Oliphant's case. These facts disclose two legal orders, both of which made incompatible claims over the same group of people (that is, the residents and institutions within the Port Madison Reservation). Moreover, as we have argued, both orders instantiate legality to a sufficient degree to be considered instances of law, properly so called. This satisfies the first three conditions for legal pluralism outlined earlier. The fourth condition remains: was there an institution with both the capacity and legitimacy to resolve the apparent conflict?

Clearly, neither the Suquamish tribal courts nor their police possessed the capacity to enforce their legal order against the contrary policy of a far more potent settler-state. Moreover, in our view, the only reasonable conclusion is that the US Supreme Court lacked legitimacy of the relevant kind. The nature of the conflict between these two orders implicated Suquamish self-determination, bringing to the fore the inequality between this Indigenous people and the settler-state within which they reside. Rather than ameliorating the injustice perpetuated by ongoing US attempts to subjugate Indian tribes, the Rehnquist Court attempted a 'disingenuous'[53] and 'performative'[54] doubling down on that oppression.[55] If this analysis holds, the necessary

51 In fact, following *Duro v Reina* 495 US 676 (1990), at least until the so-called '*Duro* fix' legislation some years later (25 USC §1301(2) (2000)), this capacity was further eroded. Under *Duro*, tribal authorities were forbidden from exercising criminal jurisdiction over *any* individual outwith their own tribes, including other Indians. A more complete attempt to dismantle tribal sovereignty through an attack on the status of Indian criminal law can scarcely be imagined.

52 In our view, this claim was legally sound and should have been upheld. The importance of public safety within the reservation, which is necessary for the enjoyment of individual autonomy and equality within that space, justified the tribal courts' power to prosecute non-Indians, which the language of the 1973 Law & Order Code supported. This position was bolstered, as we subsequently contend, by the manifest illegitimacy of Rehnquist Court's contrary ruling.

53 Duthu (n 46) 373.

54 Ball (n 40) 37.

55 This supports Peter d'Errico's allegation that 'Federal Indian Law is the continuation of colonialism', see: 'American Indian Sovereignty: Now You See It, Now You Don't' in Adolfo de Oliveira (ed), *Decolonising Indigenous Rights* (Routledge 2009) 110–11.

72 Colonial Injustice and Legal Pluralism

conclusion is one of legal pluralism, with the implication that the US must recognise and respect the continued functioning of Suquamish criminal jurisdiction on a territorial basis within the Port Madison Reservation. To see that this in fact follows, attention must be given to the illegitimacy of the Rehnquist Court itself, which has two dimensions.

First, the alleged resolution of *Oliphant* by any court belonging solely to the US legal order would have been inherently problematic. Such 'courts of the colonizer'[56] are presumptively illegitimate because demonstrating 'proper respect for tribal self-determination requires that *tribal courts* be accorded primacy in resolving any potential conflict between the tribal and [the] federal' [emphasis added].[57] As argued, the violations of autonomy and equality perpetrated by colonialism included the undermining of Indigenous self-determination. Insofar as Indigenous self-governance promoted individual autonomy, the colonial destruction and subordination of those governance practices violated that value. Furthermore, such disruption also violated equality through its asymmetry: Indigenous self-governance was undermined by settlers who, hypocritically,[58] proclaimed their own inviolable rights to political independence.[59] For contemporary settler-states, including the US, this grounds a remedial duty to facilitate the self-determination of Indigenous peoples, which sits downstream from their more general obligation to eliminate the ongoing injustices of colonial governance. Crucially, this must include presumptive non-interference with the administration of justice through Indigenous legal orders, given the importance of such orders to Indigenous self-determination.[60] In *Oliphant*, therefore, the very involvement of the US Supreme Court itself was presumptively illegitimate.[61]

---

56 Russell Barsh and James Henderson, 'The Supreme Court's Van der Peet Trilogy: Naive Imperialism and Ropes of Sand' (1996–97) 42 McGill LJ 993, 1002.

57 Duthu (n 46) 396.

58 R Jay Wallace, 'Hypocrisy, Moral Address, and Equal Standing of Persons' (2010) 38(4) Philosophy & Public Affairs 307, 309; Kyle Fritz, 'Hypocrisy, Inconsistency, and the Moral Standing of the State' (2019) 13(2) Criminal Law and Philosophy 309.

59 Thomas Jefferson and others, 'Declaration of Independence' (signed 4 July 1776).

60 This duty of non-interference *might* be limited but, we suggest, only in extreme circumstances, such as when necessary for the maintenance of civil peace and the protection of fundamental rights.

61 Indeed, it also seems likely that allowing a writ for *habeas corpus* was procedurally inappropriate under US federal law. According to the 'exhaustion' doctrine, Oliphant should have been required to exhaust tribal court remedies before such a writ could be heard. In *Oliphant*, the Supreme Court simply failed to acknowledge this established position; see Melissa Tatum, '*Oliphant v Suquamish Indian Tribe* 435 US 191 (1978) Justice Melissa L Tatum, Dissenting' in Bennett Capers, Sarah Deer, and Corey Rayburn Yung (eds), *Feminist Judgments: Rewritten Criminal Law Opinions* (CUP 2022) 75–77.

Second, attention must be given to the substance of the Supreme Court's decision: as Dworkin argues, the legitimacy of any institution always turns in part upon how it behaves.[62] Rehnquist's opinion displays three distinct violations of legality, each of which undermines its political legitimacy *vis-à-vis* the Suquamish. The first is that, as already noted, the judgement opened a prosecutorial lacuna, which generates inequality between Indians and non-Indians, insofar as only the former were recognised as being subject to tribal law. This creates problems for legality because, as we put the point elsewhere, '*no* set of criminal prohibitions can be justified *vis-à-vis* status-egalitarianism unless *all* members of the relevant polity are governed by that set and *only* that set'.[63] Conversely, '[t]o hold anyone personally exempt from regulation under the full set of criminal laws that apply to their compatriots does expressive harm to the horizontal equality that the Rule of Law maintains. Moreover . . . to single out any individual or group for *additional* criminal regulation harms civic equality in precisely the same manner' [emphasis in original].[64] But this is precisely what the Rehnquist judgement sets out to do: a system of criminal regulation exists within the Port Madison Reservation that cannot be enforced against the overwhelming majority of its resident population.[65]

The second substantive violation is that by emphasising the importance of rendering non-Indians immune from 'unwarranted intrusions on their personal liberty',[66] Rehnquist 'never addresses why non-Indians' liberty interests are privileged over those of Indians'.[67] This almost self-evidently violates the equality of Indian residents within the Port Madison Reservation and so seems flatly inconsistent with the proper application of legality, even as an 'internal' matter of US federal law. Moreover, given the acknowledged prevalence of non-Indian crime within reservations, the risk to individual Indians created by the aforementioned prosecutorial lacuna is arguably sufficient to count as an expressive violation of autonomy in its own right. This leaves aside the actual impacts of increased crime against Indian victims by non-Indian

---

62 Ronald Dworkin, *Law's Empire* (Hart Publishing 1998) 214–24.

63 Alex Green and Jennifer Hendry, '*Ad Hominem* Criminalisation and the Rule of Law: The Egalitarian Case against Knife Crime Prevention Orders' (2022) 42(2) OJLS 634, 644.

64 ibid 644–45.

65 For a full defence of defining political membership with reference to habitual residence, see: Alex Green, 'Three Models of Political Membership: Delineating "The People in Question"' (2021) 41(2) OJLS 565.

66 *Oliphant* (n 27) 210.

67 Duthu (n 46) 377; Barsh and Henderson (n 42) 635.

74 Colonial Injustice and Legal Pluralism

perpetrators,[68] the materialisation of which engenders further significant violations of autonomy.

The third violation concerns the value of maintaining legality as a systemic, albeit it partial, guarantor of political legitimacy. In addition to departing from accepted principles,[69] Rehnquist's reasoning demonstrated 'an unusual propensity for the selective use of history, assuming conclusions, and even according greater weight to defeated bills than enacted law'.[70] To quote Peter Maxfield, '[Rehnquist] drew false inferences, misrepresented or distorted case holdings and other legal authorities, and generally argued based on unsubstantiated statements . . . Would our system, so resilient yet so fragile, survive this practice on a widespread scale?'.[71] In this connection, it must be remembered that the Supreme Court is an apex appellate institution with really quite remarkable constitutional authority. The risks incurred to government by law when officials such as Rehnquist undermine the cogency of legal reasoning are far greater than those incurred by implausible legal claims from laypersons or even by relatively widespread lawbreaking amongst private individuals.[72]

Both dimensions of illegitimacy detailed here animate our finding of legal pluralism when reading *Oliphant*: a conclusion which itself bolsters the separateness of the Suquamish legal order. Seen in this light, Rehnquist's 'performative utterance'[73] that various Indigenous legal orders have been 'incorporated' into that of the US is unsupportable.[74] According to the account of legality advanced in Chapter 2, laws are customs, principles, or rules grounded upon particular kinds of governance practices. If those practices change, the content of the

---

68 That such risks exist are evident from the response from Congress in the form of the 2013 Violence Against Women Act (PL 113–14, 127 Stat 54), which restored the ability of tribal prosecutors to pursue cases against non-Indian offenders facing charges of domestic and dating violence against Indian women. See further: Shefali Singh, 'Closing the Gap of Justice: Providing Protection for Native American Women Through the Special Domestic Violence Criminal Jurisdiction of VAWA' (2014) 28(1) Columbia Journal of Gender and Law 197; Nancy Whittier, 'Carceral and Intersectional Feminism in Congress: The Violence Against Women Act, Discourse, and Policy' (2016) 30(5) Gender & Society 791; Margaret Zhang, 'Special Domestic Violence Criminal jurisdiction for Indian Tribes: Inherent Tribal Sovereignty Versus Defendants' Complete Constitutional Rights' (2015) 164 University of Pennsylvania LR 243.

69 Hendry and Tatum (n 34) 97.

70 Barsh and Henderson (n 42) 617.

71 Peter Maxfield, 'Oliphant v Suquamish Tribe: The Whole Is Greater Than the Sum of the Parts' (1993) 19 Journal of Contemporary Law 391, 443.

72 Liam Murphy, *What Makes Law: An Introduction to the Philosophy of Law* (CUP 2014) 137–39.

73 Ball (n 40) 37.

74 *Oliphant* (n 27) 209.

law is likely to change as well.[75] One way that the agents of one legal order might seek to 'incorporate' another is by dismantling the target order through the elimination of those underlying governance practices. Such 'incorporation' would be euphemistic at best, amounting to little more than the destruction of the target order. In settler-states, such destruction frequently took place, attended by injustice of the worst kind: murder, forced assimilation, coerced relocation, and enslavement, amounting to genocide.[76] The incorporation Rehnquist attempted was different. His language implied that the US absorbed the relevant Indigenous legal orders by operation of law once its territory had expanded to include that of the peoples who generated them.[77] By contrast, a finding of legal pluralism would render Rehnquist's inference conceptually impossible. As detailed in Chapter 2, since legality has strong conceptual connections to legitimacy, illegitimacy runs contrary to law's normative foundations. One implication of this is that no wholly illegitimate actions can take legal effect, even if they purport to do so by emulating legal form. To hold otherwise would commit one to the contradictory proposition that an action can both instantiate legality and simultaneously abrogate one of its underlying values. Metaphysically speaking, since there is nothing more to the existence of legality *qua* normative ideal than its substantive connections with these other values, such simultaneous instantiation and abrogation would be logically impossible.[78]

For this reason, Rehnquist's allegations of historical 'incorporation' lack any basis in law or morality. The apparent existence of a distinct Suquamish legal order and the remedial duty of the US to facilitate Suquamish self-determination together entail that no attempt at incorporation through law could have been legitimate, and therefore effective, prior to 1978. Furthermore, insofar as *Oliphant* itself represented an illegitimate attempt at incorporation, it cannot have had

---

75 Mark Greenberg, 'How Facts Make Law' in Scott Hershovitz (ed), *Exploring Law's Empire: the Jurisprudence of Ronald Dworkin* (OUP 2006) 230–40.

76 See, for example, the findings of physical, biological and cultural genocide in: The Truth and Reconciliation Commission of Canada, *Honouring the Truth, Reconciling for the Future Summary of the Final Report of the Truth and Reconciliation Commission of Canada* (2015) <http://nctr.ca/assets/reports/Final%20Reports/Executive_Summary_English_Web.pdf> last accessed 30 January 2024.

77 *Oliphant* (n 27) 209.

78 Ronald Dworkin, *Justice for Hedgehogs* (HUP 2011) 104–22. This holds, it must be emphasised, only in relation to discrete actions and not *vis-à-vis* entire legal orders: it might not be internally consistent for US law as a whole to both instantiate and abrogate legality in various different ways, but it is not logically impossible. Since law exists partly as a result of the social facts of its constitutive practices, which are themselves comprised of various acts and omissions, the instantiation of legality (and legitimacy) by any given legal order will almost always be both complex and scalar.

legal or moral effect. Importantly, neither point entails total exclusivity of operation between the US and Suquamish legal orders: the tribe's status as a sovereign dependent nation necessitates at least *some* US law operating within the Port Madison Reservation.[79] Indeed, it is partly for this reason that recognition and respect for a finding of legal pluralism is so important. Forestalled by US intervention, the Suquamish tribal authorities were prevented from addressing the conflict of jural instances raised in *Oliphant*. Conversely, no US institution, least of all the Supreme Court, possessed sufficient legitimacy to do the same. This left these two legal orders in uncomfortable and asymmetric parallel: historic injustice and considerations of legality precluded incorporation, the seeming conflict between them went without legitimate resolution, and the Supreme Court failed to acknowledge that, *qua* legal orders, both merited the same basic respect. Conversely, had the Rehnquist Court supported the separateness of the Suquamish legal order, the tribe's inherent sovereignty would have been reinforced in circumstances in which their total independence represented, from a US hegemonic perspective at least, a political nonstarter.

3.2 Giving the Mountain Time for Itself: The Cases of Mato Tipila and Uluṟu

Our next two examples concern sacred sites: one from the US and one from Australia. Such sites are instructive for understanding legal pluralism because, as Jobani and Perez observe, '[d]isputes over access, legitimate and permissible conduct, site management, and even the proper name of such sites reflect how thoroughly the understandings and meanings attributed to such sites differ'.[80] Such differences in attribution often work their way into settler-state attempts to manage (or mismanage) conflicts between the legal orders in question.[81] Moreover, given the close links between the protected promulgation of spiritual practices and

---

79 Duthu (n 46) 396–97.
80 Yuval Jobani and Nahshon Perez, 'Governing the Sacred: A Critical Typology of Models of Political Toleration in Contested Sacred Sites' (2018) 7(2) Oxford Journal of Law and Religion 250, 255.
81 For instance, notwithstanding the innovative nature of the 2014 Ruruku Whakatupua Te Mana o te Iwi o Whanganui, enacted into the law of New Zealand Aotearoa by the Te Awa Tupua (Whanganui River Claims Settlement) Act 2017, considerable potential for conflict remains: while section 14 of the Act recognises the personhood of the Whanganui River system (Te Awa Tupua), section 16a guarantees protection for preexisting property interests in the river. This holds because section 14 effectively provides a statutory basis for Māori tikanga (law), while section 16a upholds New Zealand common law rights, see *Ko Aotearoa Tēnei: A Report into Claims Concerning New Zealand Law and Policy Affecting Māori Culture and Identity*, Taumata Tuarua, Wai 262, Waitangi Tribunal Report 2011, vol 2, p 750.

the effective enjoyment of self-determination,[82] particular importance must be attached to the regulation of sacred sites.

Our first example of this kind is Mato Tipila (often translated as Bear Lodge),[83] a geological formation also known as 'Devils Tower', which stands in Wyoming's Black Hills, on the 'overlapping traditional territories of many Indian tribes of the Plains'.[84] Mato Tipila has been a US National Monument since 1906 and since 1916 has been managed by the National Park Service (NPS). Crucially for present purposes, this formation holds an important place within the belief systems and land-based religions of numerous Plains Indian tribes, over twenty of which claim a cultural affiliation with the site and still perform traditional ceremonies and rituals there.[85] Amongst these tribes, the Arapaho, Cheyenne, Crow, Kiowa, Lakota, and Shoshone all possess legal orders with features familiar to the Western-trained scholar. To take one example, the Northern Arapaho Tribe of Wyoming has a Tribal Code and Constitution,[86] with the recorded decisions of the Wind River Tribal Court appearing in the Indian Law Reporter.[87] In South Dakota, to take two further examples, the same holds of the Cheyenne River Sioux Tribe of the Cheyenne River Reservation and, amongst the Lakota peoples, the Oglala Sioux Tribe.[88] In much the same manner as those of the Suquamish legal order, the practices and institutions of these tribes are patently sufficient to instantiate legality, even discounting (as one should

82 Friederike Kelle, 'Beyond Belief: How Religion Fosters Self-Determination' (2021) 27 Nations and Nationalism 924; Ron Hassner, 'The Pessimist's Guide to Religious Coexistence' in Marshall Breger, Yitzhak Reiter, and Leonard Hammer (eds), *Holy Places in the Israeli-Palestinian Conflict: Confrontation and Co-Existence* (Routledge 2010).

83 Although Bear Lodge is the usual English translation from the commonly used Lakota name 'Mato Tipila', different Plains Indian tribes use alternative names, which can be various translated as, for example, Grey Horn Butte, Tree Rock, and The Place Where Bears Live <https://www.nps.gov/deto/learn/historyculture/aboutthename.htm> last accessed 30 January 2024.

84 Lloyd Burton and David Ruppert, 'Bear's Lodge or Devils Tower: Intercultural Relations, Legal Pluralism, and the Management of Sacred Sites on Public Land' (1999) 8(2) Cornell Journal of Law and Public Policy 201, 206.

85 Melissa Tatum and Jill Shaw, *Law, Culture & Environment* (Carolina Academic Press 2014) 62.

86 See, for example <https://northernarapaho.com/170/Tribal-Code> last accessed 30 January 2024; and National Indian Law Library <https://narf.org/nill/tribes/arapahoe_wind_river.html> last accessed 30 January 2024.

87 Wind River Tribal Court <https://www.wrtribalcourt.com/> last accessed 30 January 2024.

88 National Indian Law Library (n 86); 'Cheyenne River Sioux Tribe of the Cheyenne River Reservation, South Dakota' <https://narf.org/nill/tribes/cheyenne_river_sioux.html> last accessed 30 January 2024; National Indian Law Library, 'Oglala Sioux Tribe' <https://narf.org/nill/tribes/oglala_sioux.html> last accessed 30 January 2024.

78 Colonial Injustice and Legal Pluralism

not) those legal practices within implicated tribes less recognisable to Western-trained observers.

The spiritual importance of Mato Tipila originally led these tribes to insist upon the need for an outright ban on climbing Bear Lodge, for which it had long since been considered a premier location: over 40 years of recreational climbing have seen the rock desecrated and defaced by hundreds of metal bolts and pitons.[89] In mediating this conflict between Indigenous peoples and climbing groups, the NPS in 1992 involved key stakeholders in a working group, with the aim of creating a climbing management plan. Following three years of consultation, the final version (FCMP) was issued in 1995 and detailed, among other things, a one-month voluntary climbing closure during June, recognised as an exceptionally sacred time for the tribes. The free choice to refrain from climbing would thus be a 'personal decision' expressing 'respect for Indian people and their traditions'.[90] As a regulatory response, this might be considered particularly mild, especially given the mandatory closure of several climbing routes every year on Mato Tipila to protect nesting peregrine falcons, alongside the total ban on the use of unmanned aircraft within the park for any purpose.[91]

Nonetheless, climbers under the auspices of the Bear Lodge Multiple Use Association (BLMUA) challenged this response in the Wyoming District Court,[92] alleging that what they (somewhat mystifyingly) characterised as a 'voluntary ban' violated the Establishment Clause of the First Amendment to the US Constitution.[93] Although the District Court held that a mandatory closure would have 'depriv[ed] individuals of their legitimate use of the monument in order to enforce the tribes' rights to worship', voluntary closure could not have that effect.[94] This effectively recognised a liberty to climb Mato Tipila on behalf of the BLMUA, which was passed over largely without comment by the Tenth Circuit on appeal.[95] Conversely, notwithstanding the compromises struck by the working group, the legal orders of the affected Indigenous peoples originally mandated what in Western legal parlance might be described

---

89 Tatum and Shaw (n 85) 61.
90 Burton and Ruppert (n 84) 217.
91 National Park Service, 'Current Climbing Closures' (Devils Tower: National Monument Wyoming) <https://www.nps.gov/deto/planyourvisit/currentclimbingclosures.htm> last accessed 30 January 2024.
92 *Bear Lodge Multiple Use Association v Babbitt* 2 F.Supp.2d 1448 (D. Wyo. 1998).
93 ibid 1451.
94 ibid 1455–56.
95 *Bear Lodge Multiple Use Assoc v Babbitt* 175 F.3d 814 (10th Cir. 1999). This appeal was dismissed due to the climbers' lack of standing.

as an *erga omnes* duty not to climb their sacred site.[96] These reciprocally incompatible claims clearly represented a two-way conflict between multiple legal orders.

Useful parallels can be drawn between this conflict and our second example of Uluru, which is situated on Anangu lands in Australia's 'Red Centre', within the Uluru-Kata Tjuta National Park. Considering Uluru metaphysically inseparable from Tjukurpa, their traditional law,[97] the Aboriginal Anangu hold the 348-meter-high sandstone formation to be both an intensely sacred site and a link to 'creation ancestors'.[98] Such traditional views of the connections between law, people, and land are evocatively captured by Irene Watson, who is worth quoting on this point at length:

> Laws were birthed as were the ancestors – out of the land and the songs and stories recording our beginnings and birth connections to homelands and territories now known as Australia. Our laws are lived as a way of life, they are not written down because the knowledge of the law comes through the living of it, as law is lived, sung, danced, painted, eaten, walked upon, and loved; law lives in all things. It is law that holds the world together as it lives inside and outside of all things. The law of creation breathes life as we walk through all of its contours and valleys. It holds a continuity as there is no beginning or ending, for the constant cycles of life are held together by law.[99]

For this reason, according to Watson, typical Western conceptions of law, state, and nation must be 'exploded and expanded' if they are to

> accommodate the philosophy of Nunga [literally: Aboriginal peoples] laws: expanded to include the voices of the natural world, so that the ruwi [literally: land] of the first nations has a voice. We are not merely on and in the land, we are of it, and we speak from this place of Creation of land, of law.[100]

Understandably, this makes accurate analysis of conflicts between Indigenous legal orders and settler-state law epistemically fraught within Aboriginal contexts. Nonetheless, when considering cases like those

---

96 For example, tribal representatives 'repeatedly equated climbing the Tower to climbing St. Peter's Cathedral in Rome' (Burton and Ruppert (n 84) 214).

97 Parks Australia, 'Uluru' <https://parksaustralia.gov.au/uluru/discover/highlights/uluru/> last accessed 30 January 2024.

98 Parks Australia, 'Anangu Culture' <https://parksaustralia.gov.au/uluru/discover/culture/> last accessed 30 January 2024.

99 Watson (n 5) 254–55.

100 ibid 268.

80 Colonial Injustice and Legal Pluralism

of Uluru, good-faith attempts must be made. Unlike the compromises settled upon by NPS working group over climbing on Mato Tipila, the stated preference of the Anangu has always been for a complete ban on the recreational climbing of Uluru. By characterising it as 'a sacred place restricted by law',[101] the Anangu might be cautiously interpreted as asserting what can once more be categorised in Western terms as an *erga omnes* duty not to climb. Indeed, as Anangu traditional landowner and Board Member Tony Tjamiwa puts the point, climbing 'is not a proper part of this place'.[102]

Until a few years ago, this prohibition was more hopeful than actual, with requests to respect Anangu law and culture displayed on signs near Uluru and on the park's website.[103] As of 26 October 2019, however, the climb has closed permanently, representing a shift in Australian settler-state law to mirror the traditional requirements of Tjukurpa.[104] This came about in large part through far greater Anangu involvement in the park's management: compared to Mato Tipila, where the Indian contribution was limited to participation in the NPS working group, the Anangu share management of the national park with the Australian Government, comprising two-thirds of its Management Board. As can often be the case with the self-conscious decolonisation of political institutions,[105] the resulting shift towards recognising and respecting the binding nature of Tjukurpa is, in many respects, an archetypally justified response to the existence of legal pluralism within the settler-state context. While the Australian legal order previously provided for a liberty to climb, which overrode the preexisting requirements of Anangu law, it now acknowledges (on this point at least) the importance of non-interference with that Indigenous legal order.

---

101 Sammy Wilson, *Agenda Item Number 7a_i_Uluru* climb closure – Words from the Chair (November 2017) <https://parksaustralia.gov.au/uluru/pub/uktnp-climb-closure-words-from-chair-nov-2017.pdf> last accessed 30 January 2024.

102 Tony Tjamiwa, Uluru–Kata Tjuta National Park, *Knowledge Handbook* (Director of National Parks: Australian Government 2012) 109.

103 Parks Australia, 'Uluru Climb Closure' <https://parksaustralia.gov.au/uluru/discover/culture/uluru-climb/> last accessed 30 January 2024.

104 ibid.

105 Australia's more recent track record is less than salutary in this respect. Although a referendum was held in October 2023 on the possibility of implementing an Aboriginal and Torres Strait Islander Voice via constitutional amendment, the majority of those voting within that referendum rejected this opportunity. The Voice, as it was colloquially known, would have made recommendations to Parliament on matters affecting Aboriginal and Torres Strait Islander peoples; see National Indigenous Australians Agency, 'Referendum on an Aboriginal and Torres Strait Islander Voice' <https://www.niaa.gov.au/indigenous-affairs/referendum-aboriginal-and-torres-strait-islander-voice#voice-principle-3> last accessed 30 January 2024.

As this comparison between the treatment of sacred sites implies, the governance of Mato Tipila and Uluṟu now possess sharply contrasting moral profiles: the unchallenged ruling of the Wyoming District Court symbolically perpetuates the alleged liberty to climb Mato Tipila, while the Uluṟu-Kata Tjuṯa National Park regulations represents the normative retreat of settler-state law in favour of Tjukurpa. The latter situation is superior in terms of both political legitimacy and Indigenous self-determination. Not only does the substance of the Australian position appropriately respond to that settler-state's unjust colonial legacy, but two-thirds of the relevant decision-making body comprised Aṉangu representatives. The substance of the US position, by contrast, reinforces the hegemony of its own legal order. Moreover, as a forum, the Wyoming District Court was no less a 'court of the coloniser' – and so no less presumptively illegitimate – than the Supreme Court in *Oliphant*.

These differences generate distinct consequences in terms of legal pluralism. Whilst the Wyoming Court's decision typifies the injustices that attend failures to recognise and accommodate such pluralism, the 2019 shift in Australian policy arguably defeases the legitimacy crisis that previously surrounded Uluṟu. The illegitimacy of US courts *vis-à-vis* the Indigenous peoples connected to Mato Tipila may help to confirm the separateness of their legal orders. However, the manner in which that illegitimacy manifested – that is, through callous disregard for tribal law – simultaneously evinces problematic disrespect for those non-state orders. Furthermore, since the Wyoming Court held that a mandatory ban would constitute 'improper . . . coercion',[106] it seems unlikely that any legitimate Indigenous institution would have a realistic chance of imposing tribal law, even if their people still maintained that desire.[107] This leaves the relevant legal orders in an uncomfortable and asymmetric parallel similar to the one we identified in relation to *Oliphant*. Conversely, insofar as the Management Board of Uluṟu-Kata Tjuṯa was legitimate in issuing its climbing ban, any problematic asymmetry lapsed along with that ban's implementation. This does not imply that Tjukurpa is now somehow 'incorporated' into Australian law. Legal pluralism still pertains precisely because the ban explicitly defers to the requirements of Tjukurpa, which, at least in substance, is now the primary normative reference point governing the climbing of Uluṟu. Such issue-based deferral takes seriously Australia's duty to facilitate Aṉangu self-determination by reflecting the respect due to Tjukurpa as an independent legal order and an expression of Aṉangu collective autonomy.

---

106 *Bear Lodge Multiple Use Association* (n 92) 1455.
107 The record of the NPS working group suggests that the relevant communities no longer desire to implement a complete ban, in line with their original policies (Burton and Ruppert (n 84) 216).

4. Postcolonial Legal Pluralism

Beyond the deliberately narrow observations offered in Chapter 2, it is almost impossible to canvass the extraordinary cultural, political, and social diversity found within postcolonial states in anything other than a purely nominal manner. For this reason, beyond the obvious point that there now exists a set of formally independent states that were once administered as colonies,[108] extreme caution must be exercised before offering generalisations of any kind. Indeed, the term 'postcolonial' itself is controversial. As Ghandi indicates,

> [t]he emergence of anti-colonial and 'independent' nation-States after colonialism is frequently accompanied by a desire to forget the colonial past . . . [p]rincipally, postcolonial amnesia is symptomatic of the urge for historical self-invention . . . [i]n response, postcolonialism can be seen as a theoretical resistance to the mystifying amnesia of the colonial aftermath.[109]

For example, Fawole rejects the notion that any postindependence African state 'from that moment of the grant of flag independence, ceases to be a "colonial" state but has transitioned into a "post-colonial" one',[110] arguing instead that, generally speaking,

> most of them in reality lack legitimacy and are hardly more than rickety colonial artifacts . . . [b]ecause they are almost totally alien to the people, even the political systems and democratic institutions of the Western world that were handed over to them . . . could not be domesticated much less properly adapted for local governance.[111]

Similarly, Chatterjee avers that the 'postcolonial state in India has after all only expanded and not transformed the basic institutional arrangements of colonial law and administration, of the courts, the bureaucracy, the police, the army, and the various technical services of government'.[112] Indeed, Chatterjee goes so far as to suggest that the colonial state may not form a wholly distinctive category, on the basis that 'the history of the colonial state, far from being incidental, is of crucial interest to the

---

108 Bill Ashcroft, Gareth Griffiths, and Helen Tiffin, *Post-Colonial Studies: The Key Concepts* (Taylor & Francis 2013) 210.

109 Leela Gandhi, *Postcolonial Theory: A Critical Introduction* (Edinburgh UP 1998) 4.

110 W Alade Fawole, *The Illusion of the Post-Colonial State: Governance and Security Challenges in Africa* (Lexington Books 2018) vii.

111 ibid viii.

112 Partha Chatterjee, *The Nation and Its Fragments: Colonial and Postcolonial Histories* (Princeton UP 1993) 15.

Colonial Injustice and Legal Pluralism 83

study of the past, present, and future of the modern state',[113] because the mechanisms of coloniality themselves were and are 'part of a common strategy for the deployment of the modern forms of disciplinary power'.[114] However, it is perhaps for this very reason that the circumstances of many postcolonial states are so instructive for the study of legal pluralism. As noted in Chapter 2, the position of non-hegemonic legal orders within postcolonial contexts can be normatively complex, since it is not only those orders themselves but also the larger set of individuals nominally represented by the relevant hegemonic state legal orders that have histories of subordination to colonial rule. Unlike the case of CANZUS settler-states, where the appropriate reaction to legal pluralism is almost always state retreat, permitting Indigenous self-determination and expressing appropriate respect for the operation of non-state law, the same will not necessarily hold where a postcolonial state is itself attempting to pursue self-determination as a discrete political community in the shadow of its own decolonisation.

4.1 In Search of Common Ground: Customary Law and Land Conflicts

The normative complexity of postcolonial legal pluralism belies the trend, particularly within scholarship on postcolonial Africa, towards 'a society centric approach as opposed to a state centric approach'.[115] Gebeye critiques the resulting 'ambition to advocate for a bifurcated theory of law' as obfuscating of both 'the role and place of the state in society . . . [and that of] traditional authorities . . . in the functioning of colonial states and the continuous viability of post-colonial states'.[116] We concur, up to a point. Many African states exhibit what Merry refers to as 'classic legal pluralism',[117] whereby customary and religious law not only intersects with but is also recognised and utilised by the state. For instance, in the Republic of Burundi, state law

> withdraws and ultimately refers civil cases to customary concili- ation processes when judgments emanating from the State justice system cannot be enforced on the ground without conciliation before the bashingantahe [literally: wise men], who thus bear the *de*

---

113 ibid 18.
114 ibid.
115 Berihun Gebeye, 'Decoding Legal Pluralism in Africa' (2017) 49(2) Journal of Legal Pluralism & Unofficial Law 228, 230.
116 ibid 230–33.
117 Sally Merry, 'Legal Pluralism' (1988) 22(5) Law and Society Review 869, 872.

facto responsibility of finding an outcome that is acceptable to the parties.[118]

Similarly, in the Republic of Zambia, paragraph 7(d) of the 2016 Constitution holds customary law consistent with the provisions of its own text to form part of the Zambian legal order.[119] In one sense, this 'incorporation by authorisation' of traditional customary law mirrors the coercively effective but ultimately unjustified allegations of normative supremacy made by officials of the US legal order *vis-à-vis* Indigenous law within that jurisdiction. The Zambian Constitution, which, in this respect, is broadly representative of similar documents throughout postcolonial Africa,[120] also purports to render void all customary law and practices not consistent with its text.[121] However, no CANZUS state relies upon the reciprocal operation of non-state law to secure social control to the same extent found within some African postcolonial jurisdictions. As such, nominal declarations of absolute superiority within this context must be treated with some caution.

This need for caution is unscored by the fact that, as Tamanaha argues, the appearance and identification of traditional customary principles within state-recognised courts necessarily differs from the existence that those same principles may possess within more socially embedded contexts.[122] Within small communities, closely united by cultural, spiritual, and other traditions, a customary principle may exhibit the horizontal qualities of legality by serving as a unifying standard for behaviour while at the same time exhibiting a degree of flexibility that 'from the standpoint of Western legal systems . . . sounds defective'.[123] As Comaroff and Roberts detail, 'indigenous rules are not seen as a priori "laws" that have the capacity to determine the outcome of disputes in a straightforward fashion . . . the rules may themselves be the object of negotiation'.[124] Moreover, within communities of this kind, where '[s]trict rule application results in winners and losers . . . dialogue and negotiation [of the type afforded by more flexible standards] encourages acceptance',[125] autonomy is arguably better served by restoring peace

---

118 Ghislain Otis, Jean Leclair, and Sophie Thériault, *Applied Legal Pluralism: Processes, Driving Forces and Effects* (Routledge 2023) 50.

119 Constitution of Zambia (1991) No. 1 of 1991 (revised 2016).

120 Gebeye (n 115) 241. See, for example, The Constitution of the Republic of Ghana (1992), section 1(2).

121 Constitution of Zambia (n 119) para 1.

122 Brian Tamanaha, 'Legal Pluralism Across the Global South: Colonial Origins and Contemporary Consequences' (2021) 53(2) Journal of Legal Pluralism & Unofficial Law 168, 176–79.

123 ibid 177.

124 John Comaroff and Simon Roberts, *Rules and Processes: The Cultural Logic of Dispute in an African Context* (University of Chicago Press 1992) 13–14.

125 Tamanaha (n 122) 177.

and harmonious relations than it would be by the more impersonal and adversarial models that facilitate that value within far larger and more anonymising 'Westphalian' political communities.[126] Legality, as we emphasised, must always be applied within the appropriate context, and scholars should hesitate before importing cultural and social presuppositions ill-suited to communities different from their own. The resulting differences between the normative content and implications of customary law as it appears within postcolonial state institutions and 'living customary law',[127] as it is practiced outwith such institutions, further reinforces the hesitance one should feel before accepting state-centric discourses of incorporation at face value.

Nowhere is this clearer than in relation to conflicts that arise in relation to land use. State legal orders within Africa formally recognise between just two and ten percent of customary land rights within that continent's overall landmass.[128] On the one hand, many African states rely upon customary legal orders and non-state dispute resolution processes to maintain land governance within territory over which they have relatively little direct control.[129] On the other, where state law exerts itself over areas also governed by customary standards, individuals relying upon these non-state legal orders frequently experience considerable insecurity, as their land rights may be either misunderstood, overlooked, or rejected outright.[130] Once again taking the example of Zambia, 'the complex customary and statutory

---

126 This is not to suggest that such governance is entirely ad hoc: even flexible customary principles function to restrain collective decision-making by requiring participants to communicate through a shared normative framework. Tamanaha emphasises that 'informal village tribunals' operate in a context in which 'those who preside in the tribunal and those involved in the dispute are familiar with one another, with multiple ongoing connections, and share a past and future together within the community . . . [and s]ince they are from the same community, furthermore, [these] people are familiar with the . . . applicable norms' (ibid 179). In these circumstances, the vertical dimension of legality can be instantiated notwithstanding what might be perceived, from a Western standpoint, as a considerable lack of formality.

127 Gordon Woodman, 'A Survey of Customary Laws in Africa in Search of Lessons for the Future' in Jeanmarie Fenrich, Paolo Galizzi, and Tracy Higgins (eds), *The Future of African Customary Law* (CUP 2011) 24–25, 27.

128 Klaus Deininger, 'Monitoring and Evaluation of Land Policies and Land Reform' in Hans Binswanger-Mkhize, Camille Bourguignon, and Rogier van den Brink (eds), *Agricultural Land Redistribution: Towards Greater Consensus* (The Word Bank 2009) 401–2.

129 Gebeye (n 115) 231, 242–43.

130 Tamanaha (n 122) 186. For detailed analysis of this trend in, for example, the Ugandan context, see: Irene Namae, 'Theoretical Recognition of Indigenous Self-Determination against Practical Implementation: A Case of the Batwa in Uganda' (SJD thesis, University of Arizona 2023) 51–60, 124–35, 141–64. In a comparative vein, see: Amrita Mukherjee, 'Customary Law and Land Rights: The Cautionary Tale of India, Jharkhand, and the Chotanagpur Tenancy Act' in Jennifer Hendry and others (eds), *Indigenous Justice: New Tools, Approaches, and Spaces* (Palgrave MacMillan 2018).

86 Colonial Injustice and Legal Pluralism

systems' governing land tenure '[i]n practice, [create] diverging interests, perceptions, overlapping power struggles, legitimacy and authority amongst the two land tenure systems, [which] have affected enjoyment of land access, control and ownership'.[131] Under Zambian state law, land rights are regulated by legislation such as The 1994 Lands Deeds and Registry Act governs,[132] whereas '[u]nder customary land tenure, land [is] allocated to subjects by chiefs [and] affords them powers to exercise control', the precise manifestations of which depend upon locality and can vary considerably in terms of the nature and scope of the rights in question. [133] The ascertainment and management of conflicts between these two modes of land regulation are frequently exacerbated by adjudicative difficulties applying customary laws, given both their unwritten nature and the local interests implicated in their identification.[134]

These difficulties are compounded by the fact that colonial 'indirect rule' often coopted and altered Indigenous authority structures, making it challenging to ascertain the extent to which some customary traditions originate from the authentic practices of those living on the land. For example, within the Ghanian context, Schmid argues that '[t]he idea that people might be able to rely without major adaptations on authentic indigenous law, sometimes with the connotation of an untainted precolonial law, remain[s] an illusion'.[135] To this end, Schmid draws a malleable distinction between 'traditional law', which is largely a product of self-interested colonial artifice and manipulation by powerful groups within the postcolonial state,[136] and 'folk law', which arises from an autonomous social field and 'determines most parts of [Ghanian] legal

---

131 Dimuna Phiri, 'A Legal Analysis of Disjunctions between Statutory and Customary Land Tenure Regimes in Zambia' (2022) 54(1) Legal Pluralism and Critical Social Analysis 96, 98.

132 Other relevant instruments include the Land Acquisition Act (1970), the Lands Act (1995), the Water Management Resources Act (2011), and the Urban and Regional Planning Act (2015).

133 Phiri (n 131) 100, 103.

134 Tamanaha (n 122) 178. For analysis of the same problem in a different context, see: Dirk Kolff, 'The Indian and the British Law Machines: Some Remarks on Law and Society in British India' in Wolfgang Mommsen and Jaap de Moor (eds), *European Expansion and Law: The Encounter of European and Indigenous Law in 19th- and 20th-Century Africa and Asia* (Berg Publishers 1992) 230–31.

135 Ulrike Schmid, 'Legal Pluralism as a Source of Conflict in Multi-Ethnic Societies: The Case of Ghana' (2001) 46 Journal of Legal Pluralism and Unofficial Law 1, 13.

136 ibid 18–21, 31–33. For analysis of a similar strategy within Apartheid South Africa, see: Barbara Oomen, 'Group Rights in Post-apartheid South Africa: The Case of Traditional Leaders' (1999) 44 Journal of Legal Pluralism & Unofficial Law 73, 86–89; William Beinart and Saul Dubow (eds), *Segregation and Apartheid in Twentieth-Century South Africa* (Routledge 1995); Ivan Evans, *Bureaucracy and Race: Native Administration in South Africa* (University of California Press 1997).

reality'.[137] That contrast is exemplified within Ghana by the 1991 challenges made by the Nawuri people, a relatively small ethnic community within the Traditional Area of the larger and more powerful Gonja, over recognition of title to their land and the authority of their chiefs. According to Schmid's historical analysis, the customary rights of allodial title claimed by the Paramount Chiefs of the Gonja over the disputed Kpandai land were largely a product of the colonial rearrangement of power between these two peoples.[138]

Situations such as these meet each of the conditions for legal pluralism established in Chapter 2. The intersecting promulgation of parallel state and non-state legal practices within postcolonial land regulation observably results in multiple governance traditions making normative claims over the same sets of people. Moreover, these state and non-state orders characteristically exhibit the value of legality to some non-negligible degree: any collection of general (albeit flexible) principles that addresses coordination problems in relation to the use of land will enhance autonomy and instantiate equality, albeit of a largely formal kind.[139] Admittedly, the degree to which each value is reflected within a particular set of governance practices will vary. There are well-documented concerns, for example, about the conflicts that arise between particular customary legal orders and the protection of human rights[140] as well as between those same orders and the equal concern and respect that is due to women.[141] But, like any other value, the instantiation of legality is scalar, meaning that many imperfectly egalitarian state and customary orders will fall within an acceptable range on that scale.[142] If one accepts that Western states, with their own histories of patriarchy, racism, and heteronormativity (to name but a few such ills), nonetheless possess the Rule

---

137 Schmid (n 135) 13. This mirror's Tamanaha's usage, see: Brian Tamanaha, 'Scientific versus Folk Legal Pluralism' (2021) 53(3) Journal of Legal Pluralism & Unofficial Law 427.

138 Schmid (n 135) 18–21, 23–31. Allodial title consists in 'interests of benefit' and 'interests of control', where the former concerns rights to exploit the land in question and the latter the power to determine who holds rights of exploitation, see: Antony Allott, 'Towards a Definition of Absolute Ownership' (1961) 5 Journal of African Law 99.

139 Immanuel Kant, *The Metaphysics of Morals* (Mary Gregor tr, CUP 2017) 54–55, 89–90.

140 Tamanaha (n 122) 188–91.

141 Mulela Munalula, 'Law as an Instrument of Social Change: The Constitution and Sexual Discrimination in Zambia' (1995) 1 International Journal Discrimination & Law 131, 137.

142 Jeremy Waldron, *One Another's Equals: The Basis of Human Equality* (Belknap Press 2017) 125–30.

of Law,[143] analogous injustices within non-Western contexts must be treated consistently.

This being so, and given the equally well-documented nature of conflicting beliefs about entitlements to land in postcolonial contexts,[144] what remains to be assessed is the presence or absence of some legitimate body with the capacity to resolve these disputes. As should be clear from our foregoing discussion, in very many cases, there are none. Postcolonial state institutions either lack the capacity to enforce their laws over disputed lands or are suspect in terms of their normative credentials. As Schmid notes, 'the socio-cultural foreignness of the normative legal order of the modern state, which is, despite adaptations by the postcolonial state, a legacy from colonial times, adds to . . . popular alienation'.[145] This tension, which, in large part, can be viewed as one of collective self-determination, claimed in particular by those reinforcing alternative normative lifeworlds by mediating their differences through non-state law, is exacerbated by 'the inadequacy of the material resources disposed of by state structures . . . [and] the corruption and lack of responsiveness of the actors and institutions of the modern state'.[146] Moreover, in many cases, as already noted, 'the deeper structures of the colonial legal and political order were inherited or, in some cases, reorganised, to reinforce despotism in the post-independence period'.[147] In this way, although postcolonial states are neither identical with nor direct continuations of preexisting colonial institutions in the manner that many settler-states are, the fact that they are nonetheless often their inheritors weakens their internal legitimacy along analogous lines.

Conversely, it is by no means always clear that traditional leaders are any better placed, at least in general terms, to resolve apparent conflicts between state and non-state law. Materially, such leaders characteristically lack the power to oppose the contrary application of state law.[148] Moreover, in cases in which land is disputed between two or more ethnic

---

143 For an extended analysis of one such problem within English and Welsh law, see: Green and Hendry (n 63).

144 In the Republic of Kenya, for example, it is commonplace for disputes to be taken to both state and customary tribunals, with different results ensuing, see: Jürg Helbling, Walter Kälin, and Prosper Nobirabo, 'Access to Justice, Impunity and Legal Pluralism in Kenya' (2015) 47(2) Journal of Legal Pluralism & Unofficial Law 347.

145 Schmid (n 135) 9.

146 ibid.

147 Issa Shivji, 'State and Constitutionalism: A New Democratic Perspective' in Issa Shivji (ed), *State and Constitutionalism: An African Debate on Democracy* (SAPES Trust 1991) 29.

148 For a detailed study of the power and influence of Chiefs in Zambia, see: Wim van Binsbergen, 'Chiefs and the State in Independent Zambia: Exploring the Zambian National Press' (1987) 25–26 Journal of Legal Pluralism & Unofficial Law 139.

Colonial Injustice and Legal Pluralism   89

groups, the traditional leaders of these groups are often suspected of bias by the other implicated peoples, which sometimes pushes disputes back into the hands of the state.[149] It is also not uncommon for traditional leaders themselves to be accused of bribery, corruption, and abuses of power.[150] Finally, there are 'traditional' structures of power within post-colonial states, such as those between the Nawuri and Gonja peoples, which exist as much due to colonial intervention as to Indigenous prac-tice. Leaders with customary authority in situations like these may well have inherited that authority from arrangements adopted under the aus-pices of colonial powers, which to that extent renders their political legit-imacy no less suspect than that of postcolonial state institutions which willingly adopted colonial governance practices. With this in view, the otherwise understandable tendency to believe that traditional leaders as a set are *necessarily* best place to determine important disputes in which two or more different legal orders are implicated must be treated with a certain reserve. The finding of legal pluralism justified by these com-monplace difficulties in locating a sufficiently powerful and legitimate decision-maker helps us diagnose the values at stake within disputes of this kind, even if (unlike in the case of settler-states) it offers no clear path forward on its own.

4.2 Unseen Peoples: Postcolonial Legal Pluralism and the Complicity of International Law

So far, we have examined conflicts between two or more legal orders that turn on the incompatibility of reasonably discrete sets of jural instances. Within the settler-state context, we examined liabilities to tribal prosecution and alleged liberties to access sacred sites, and in relation to postcolonial states, we have so far focused upon land use conflicts. In this final part, we examine more abstract conflicts identi-fiable at a grander scale: those between international law and the moral necessity to recognise on equal terms independent non-state legal orders as means for Indigenous self-determination. As noted in Chapter 2, contemporary international law recognises that the total

---

149 Rasmus Pedersen, 'State-Orchestrated Access to Land Dispute Settlement in Africa: Land Conflicts and New-Wave Land Reform in Tanzania' in Olaf Zenker and Virgil Markus (eds), *The State and the Paradox of Customary Law in Africa* (Routledge 2018) 177.
150 Jarle Simensen, 'Jurisdiction as Politics: The Gold Coast during the Colonial Period' in Wolfgang Mommsen and Jaap de Moor (eds), *European Expansion and Law: The Encounter of European and Indigenous Law in 19th- and 20th-Century Africa and Asia* (Berg Publishers 1992) 271–72; Janine Ubink, 'Traditional Authority Revisited: Popular Perceptions of Chiefs and Chieftaincy in Peri' (2007) 39(55) Journal of Legal Pluralism & Unofficial Law 123.

set of peoples with a right to self-determination is not limited to the populations of recognised states but also includes various non-state groups. Nonetheless, states possess an elevated status within the international legal order that privilege them as self-determination units. For example, only states possess the right to full political independence, which is characterised in international law as freedom from 'inter-governmental domination'.[151] Similarly, it is states, and not the Indigenous or other minority groups that live within them, which possess the right to hold territory, whether the territorial unit in question is maritime or land based.[152] To take just one more example, although the nominal beneficiaries of the permanent sovereignty over natural resources are peoples,[153] in practice, the right to dispose freely of the natural wealth within a particular territory accrues to states as territorial title holders.[154]

This being so, although it has been argued that 'full self-determination, in a real sense, does not require or justify a separate state',[155] others have contended that 'self-determination is, at the most basic level, a principle concerned with the right to be a State'.[156] The truth is probably somewhere in between these two extremes. Although peoples without

151 Green (n 1) 87.
152 *Island of Palmas (Netherlands v United States of America) (Award)* (1928) 2 RIAA 829, 838. Some non-state entities have possessed territorial title; however, this is very much an exception and requires particular legal authorisation, see for example: SC Res 1272 (1999) UN Doc S/RES/1272.
153 UNGA Res 1803(XVII) (1962) A/RES/1803(XVII) para 1 (attributing the right to peoples and States); International Covenant on Civil and Political Rights (ICCPR) (signed 16 December 1966, entered into force 23 March 1976) 999 UNTS 173, art 47; International Covenant on Economic, Social and Cultural Rights (ICESCR) (signed 16 December 1966, entered into force 3 January 1976) 993 UNTS 3, art 25; African Charter on Human and Peoples' Rights (adopted and entered into force 26 June 1981) 1520 UNTS 217, art 21(1); United Nations Declaration on the Rights of Indigenous Peoples (UNDRIP), UNGA Res 61/295 (2007) UN Doc A/RES/61/295, art 8(b); Nicolaas Schrijver, 'Self-Determination of Peoples and Sovereignty Over Natural Wealth and Resources' in *Realizing the Right to Development Essays in Commemoration of 25 Years of the United Nations Declaration on the Right to Development* (United Nations 2013); Emeka Duruigbo, 'Permanent Sovereignty and Peoples' Ownership of Natural Resources in International Law' (2006) 38 George Washington International LR 33, 54; JN Hyde, 'Permanent Sovereignty Over Natural Wealth and Resources' (1956) 50 AJIL 854.
154 UNGA Res 1314(XIII) (1958) UN Doc A/RES/1314(XIII); *Armed Activities on the Congo (Democratic Republic of the Congo v Uganda) (Merits)* [2005] ICJ Rep 168, para 244; *East Timor (Portugal v Australia) (Merits)* [1995] ICJ Rep 90, Dissenting Opinion of Judge Weeramantry, 111–13; UNGA Res 3201(S-VI) (1974) UN DOC A/RES/3201(S-IV); UNGA Res 3281(XXIX) (1974) UN Doc A/RES/3281(XXIX); UNGA Res 41/128 (1997) UN Doc A/41/128.
155 S James Anaya, *Indigenous Peoples in International Law* (OUP 2004) 7.
156 James Crawford, *The Creation of States in International Law* (OUP 2007) 107.

their own states can achieve significant self-determination within larger political communities, 'some change in existing structures of governance or other measures short of secession are needed to bring about and ensure an atmosphere in which they may live and develop freely, under conditions of equality in all spheres of life'.[157] Conversely, international law's history of denying equal status to various non-European peoples is inseparable from its practices of statehood and state recognition.[158] This can be seen from Indigenous experiences of colonialism, in which the very existence of several peoples was effectively denied in order to facilitate European colonisation of their traditional lands. To quote Watson on the Australian context:

> Muldarbi [literally: demon spirit] law said that the Australian continent was clothed with a blanket of terra nullius of the land, law and people. The Nunga subject in law was deemed not to exist. We were instead defined as British subjects, but subjects without the legal status of British subjects. Nunga laws thereby became covered by the rules and regulations, part of the muldarbi's colonial project of genocide.[159]

International law is complicit in this practice of genocide through its insistence upon Westphalian forms of statehood and sovereignty. As Green argues, by 'unseeing' Indigenous peoples in this manner, international law mirrors more day-to-day rejections of social and political reality, such as 'our refusal to "see" the homeless[, which] stems from our dread of acknowledging the structural injustices that construct destitution: injustices in which we are all participants, whether knowingly or otherwise'.[160] Such unseeing, he contends, was entirely strategic on the part of European states because:

> [G]enocide cannot be perpetrated against non-existent communities, making the European colonial project's unseeing of Aboriginal Australians the most desperate and total form of ethical self-preservation imaginable. Just as you and I preserve the illusion of our ethical selves by unseeing the destitute and downtrodden, so Europe preserved its illusions of justice and entitlement by manufacturing a false 'destruction of nothing'. But its ethical self-destruction was inescapable: by

---

157   Anaya (n 155) 8.
158   Alex Green, 'Towards an Impossible Polis: Legal Imagination and State Continuity' in Alex Green, Mitchell Travis, and Kieran Tranter (eds), *Science Fiction as Legal Imaginary* (Routledge 2025).
159   Watson (n 5) 17.
160   Green (n 158).

unseeing in order to excuse, genocide was multiplied rather than avoided. To deny the status of our victims is, at least figuratively, already to destroy them; it adds, as it were, an ultimate insult to the ultimate injury.[161] [References omitted.]

This is not only of historical interest. In her legally pluralist reading of the *Bakassi Peninsula* case,[162] Hendry argues that the International Court of Justice (ICJ), largely due to the limitations of its inter-state jurisdiction,[163] failed adequately to account for 'the *people* of Bakassi, 90% of who are Nigerians of the indigenous Efik tribe. Overlooked amidst the dispute over territory, the Efik people's way of life – by and large sustained until 2008 in spite of the historical impact of colonial rule – was brought to an end by the implementation of the ICJ's ruling' [emphasis in original].[164] The territorial dispute in question was between the Republic of Cameroon and the Federal Republic of Nigeria, concerning title over certain areas of Lake Chad and the Peninsula of Bakassi itself.[165] In ruling on that dispute, the ICJ found that title rested with Cameroon,[166] the practical upshot of which was that the Efik had to 'either take Cameroonian nationality or retain Nigerian nationality and become foreigners in their ancestral homeland'.[167] By relying on a conception of legal pluralism that utilises a 'subject-driven, bottom-up conceptualisation of law [which] empowers . . . subjects by vesting their lived experiences with legal relevance',[168] Hendry contends that the state-centric nature of much international dispute resolution creates a 'jurisdictional blindspot', preventing peoples like the Efik from being treated on equal terms with those of larger, formally recognised polities.[169] This, in turn, denies them the agency over their collective fates that forms the *sine qua non* of self-determination.[170]

Unlike the more discrete clashes of jural instances examined here, these practices of 'unseeing' peoples outwith the Westphalian paradigm directly evidence a blanket existential conflict between international

---

161 ibid.
162 *Land and Maritime Boundary between Cameroon and Nigeria (Cameroon v Nigeria: Equatorial Guinea intervening) (Merits)* [2002] ICJ Rep 303.
163 Jennifer Hendry, 'A Legally Pluralist Approach to the *Bakassi Peninsula* Case' in Damian Gonzalez-Salzberg and Loveday Hodson (eds), *Research Methods for International Human Rights Law: Beyond the Traditional Paradigm* (Routledge 2020) 133.
164 ibid 131.
165 Hendry (n 163) 316–25.
166 ibid 402–9, 454–58.
167 ibid, citing: *Bakassi Resettlement Commission Report* (2009), Governor's Office, Calabar, Cross River State.
168 Hendry (n 163) 125.
169 ibid 135–36.
170 ibid 136–40.

law on the one hand and various Indigenous and other non-state legal orders on the other. As argued in Chapter 2, the promulgation of an independent legal order provides one profound way in which peoples can collectively self-determine. By rejecting parity between state and non-state legal orders, international law thereby denies parity between the self-determination of non-state peoples and that of peoples who can be defined through either their legal nationality or their residence within a particular state.[171] This can be seen, for example, in Kelsen's seemingly unmotivated discrimination between the two when he defines statehood itself in terms of law:

> As a political organization, the state is a legal order. But not every legal order is a state . . . The state is a relatively centralized legal order . . . The legal order of primitive society and the general international law order are entirely decentralized coercive orders and therefore not states. In traditional theory the state is composed of three elements, the people of the state, the territory of the state, and the so-called power of the state, exercised by an independent government. All three elements can be determined only juridically, that is, they can be comprehended only as the validity and the spheres of validity of a legal order.[172]

Such discrimination between self-determining peoples is difficult to explain in moral terms, such that no plausible, good-faith justification of the state-centric nature of international law could ever be more than provisional.[173] Nonetheless, the presence of legal pluralism is clear. International law *does* exhibit many important features of legality, including an intelligible conception of equality,[174] a fundamental concern with human rights and the dignity of persons (implying at least some instantiation of autonomy),[175] and several legitimacy-enhancing functions in relation to the legal orders of established states.[176] To this extent, international law must be considered law, properly so called.

---

171 For the distinction between these two, see: Crawford (n 156) 52–55.
172 Hans Kelsen, *The Pure Theory of Law* (Max Knight tr, 2nd edn, California UP 1967) 286–87. See also: Krystyna Marek, *Identity and Continuity of States in Public International Law* (Librairie Droz 1968) 168, 188.
173 Green (n 1) 11–12.
174 Alex Green, 'A Political Theory of State Equality' (2023) 14(2) Transnational Legal Theory 178.
175 Ratner (n 15) 64–103; Patrick Capps, *Human Dignity and the Foundations of International Law* (Hart Publishing 2009).
176 Ronald Dworkin, 'A New Philosophy for International Law' (2013) 41(1) Philosophy & Public Affairs 2.

That it is in apparent conflict with various non-state legal orders within postcolonial spaces can be seen *a fortiori* for two reasons. First, as we argue, many such orders exhibit significant features of the Rule of Law in contextually salient ways. Second, it follows from the nature of legality that each independent legal order must, in the absence of external interference, aspire to enhance autonomy, equality, and legitimacy within the confines of a jurisdiction established by its constitutive governance practices. It follows from *this* that each such order must claim, through the individuals that its own customs, principles, or rules designate as speaking for it,[177] some degree of practical authority to the exclusion of other orders of the same kind.[178] This must hold, therefore, for state and non-state legal orders alike. Now, subject to particular restraints, such as the protection of human rights,[179] international law endorses state sovereignty, which is commonly understood as 'plenary authority to administer territory'.[180] Given that most contemporary states exercise the vast preponderance of this authority through their legal orders, this entails that international law both acknowledges and accepts that state law in fact possesses a substantial degree of the practical authority that it claims. However, as can be seen from cases like *Bakassi Peninsula*, the same does not hold for non-state legal orders. International law remains coldly indifferent to the practical authority claims made by orders of this kind, especially where they are not asserted within territorial bounds but in line with jurisdictions that are, for example, ethnic or filial.[181] Such state-centric partiality amounts to an implicit but fundamental rejection of the legality that attaches to these non-state governance traditions. That is a conflict *par excellence*.

Turning now to the question of sufficiently powerful and legitimate adjudicators for the resolution of this conflict, it is equally clear that there are none. The ICJ itself is incapable of hearing complaints from non-state entities.[182] Moreover, by this very token, it is complicit in 'the ideology of state centrism, which is to say, the idea of law as operating only top-down, as something that *acts upon* society' [emphasis in

---

177 John Gardener, 'How Law Claims, What Law Claims' in Matthias Klatt (ed), *Institutionalized Reason: The Jurisprudence of Robert Alexy* (OUP 2012) 29–33.
178 ibid 34–35.
179 Capps (n 175) 264–65; Evan Criddle and Evan Fox-Decent, *Fiduciaries of Humanity: How International Law Constitutes Authority* (OUP 2016) 76, 194.
180 Crawford (n 156) 32(n.140).
181 Hendry (n 163) 142–43; Basil Davidson, *Old Africa Rediscovered* (Longman 1967) 337; Mark Funteh, 'The Concept of Boundary and Indigenous Application in Africa: The Case of the Bakassi Boarder Lines of Cameroon and Nigeria' (2015) 1(4) International Journal of Humanities and Cultural Studies 220, 224.
182 Statute of the International Court of Justice, 18 April 1946, art 34(1).

original].[183] The same applies to other major United Nations bodies, such as the General Assembly and the Security Council, who might pass resolutions on the matter. This is no mere hypothetical point. For example, although General Assembly resolution 1514(XV) provides that '[a]ll peoples have the right to self-determination; by virtue of that right they freely determine their political status and freely pursue their economic, social and cultural development',[184] it also holds that '[a]ny attempt aimed at the partial or total disruption of the national unity and the territorial integrity of a country is incompatible with the purposes and principles of the Charter of the United Nations'.[185] This, as Hendry argues, implies that 'this Resolution was intended to support nascent states, instead of providing a genuinely restorative mechanism for people(s) negatively affected by colonial violence'.[186] For much the same reason, the international community of states acting outwith any international organisation, although sufficiently powerful and ultimately responsible for questions of status and recognition under international law,[187] are far too clearly judges in their own case to possess the necessary legitimacy. To be clear, our point is not that states should refrain from exercising their legal authority, on either an individual or collective basis,[188] to promote equitable arrangements for the greater recognition of non-state legal orders and the further self-determination of Indigenous peoples. Justice demands no less. Our objection is only

183 Hendry (n 163) 135.
184 UNGA Res 1514(XV) (1960) UN Doc A/Res/1514(XV), para 2.
185 ibid para 6.
186 Hendry (n 163) 137. This conclusion *might* be somewhat muted by the text of UNGA Res 2625(XXV) (1974) UN Doc A/RES/2625(XXV), principle 5, which holds that the 'subjection of peoples to alien subjugation, domination and exploitation' violates self-determination and that '[e]very State has the duty to refrain from any forcible action which deprives peoples . . . of their right to self-determination and freedom and independence'. While it is true that principle 5 also stipulates that '[n]othing in the foregoing paragraphs shall be construed as authorizing or encouraging any action which would dismember or impair, totally or in part, the territorial integrity or political unity of sovereign and independent States', this is subject to the qualification that those states must conduct 'themselves in compliance with the equal rights and the self-determination of peoples as described above and thus possessed of a government representing the whole people belonging to the territory without distinction as to race, creed or colour'. As our argument implies, international practice in support of expansive readings of this qualification is thin on the ground. Nonetheless, such arguments are at least possible. As Green has contended elsewhere, for example, a limited right to remedial secession exists in contemporary international law notwithstanding the premium placed upon territorial integrity, see: Green (n 1) 132–36.
187 Hersch Lauterpacht, *Recognition in International Law* (CUP 2012) 55.
188 Fine questions persist as to how this might be achieved, especially given the otherwise supportable requirements of state consent for any action taken in relation to their respective territories. We remain deliberately agnostic on these questions here, with the exception of noting the importance of participation by non-state peoples.

96 Colonial Injustice and Legal Pluralism

that states cannot legitimately exercise that authority alone: the respect due to both non-state law and peoples requires the full and free participation of all the peoples involved under conditions of equality and mutual respect.[189]

5. Conclusion

In this chapter, we canvassed several instances of legal pluralism that fit the account of that phenomenon advanced in Chapter 2. We began by outlining the ways in which the injustice of colonialism complicates the challenges of political legitimacy and Indigenous self-determination within settler and postcolonial states. Using this more general argument, we established why states of both types provide fertile ground for legal pluralism to flourish. Drawing upon conflicts within the administration of criminal justice, those concerning the use and reverence due to sacred sites, and others surrounding the regulation of land, we demonstrated how sets of seemingly incompatible jural instances can be used to confirm the existence of legal pluralism within a range of settings affected by the injustice of colonialism. Moreover, approaching matters at a grander scale, we identified the complicity not only of settler-state and postcolonial law but also of international law in the ongoing subjugation of Indigenous legal orders. By interrogating legal pluralism in this normatively engaged manner, we brought to the fore

---

189 Much can be learned, we would argue, from the participatory model adopted during the drafting of UNDRIP, despite its complex and often contentious nature. See, for example: Sharon Venne, 'The Road to the United Nations and the Rights of Indigenous Peoples' (2011) 20 Giffith LR 557; Les Malezer, 'Dreamtime Discovery: New Reality and Hope' in Jackie Hartley, Paul Joffe, and Jennifer Preston (eds), *Realizing the UN Declaration on the Rights of Indigenous Peoples: Triumph, Hope and Action* (Purich 2010); Kenneth Deer, 'Reflections on the Development, Adoption, and Implementation of the UN Declaration on the Rights of Indigenous Peoples' in Jackie Hartley, Paul Joffe, and Jennifer Preston (eds), *Realizing the UN Declaration on the Rights of Indigenous Peoples: Triumph, Hope and Action* (Purich 2010); Luis Enrique Chavez, 'The Declaration on the Rights of Indigenous Peoples Breaking the Impasse: The Middle Ground' in Claire Charters and Rodolfo Stavenhagen (eds), *Making the Declaration Work: the United Nations Declaration on the Rights of Indigenous Peoples* (Transaction 2009); Andrea Carmen, 'International Indian Treaty Council Report from the Battle Field – The Struggle for the Declaration' in Claire Charters and Rodolfo Stavenhagen (eds), *Making the Declaration Work: the United Nations Declaration on the Rights of Indigenous Peoples* (Transaction 2009); Megan Davis, 'United Nations Declaration on the Rights of Indigenous Peoples' (2008) 9 Melbourne Journal of International Law 439; Julian Burger, 'Standard-setting: Lessons Learned for the Future' (Paper presented at the International Council on Human Rights Policy and International Commission of Jurists Workshop, Geneva, 13–14 February 2005) 7; Megan Davis, 'The United Nations Draft Declaration 2002' (2002) 5(16) Indigenous Law Bulletin 6.

the intricate moral profiles of societies grappling with colonial legacies, in which law, far from playing a dry and formal role, sits at the heart of ongoing moral and political tensions concerning issues of group identity, institutional injustice, and the construction of multiple and contested lifeworlds within which diverse peoples pursue their collective destinies.

Conclusion
The Universal Plurality of Law

Following the intellectual history outlined in Chapter 1, Chapters 2 and 3 argued that legal pluralism is not just an undeniable social reality but also an important moral phenomenon that carries crucial implications for political legitimacy and collective self-determination within a range of different contexts. Characteristically, to recognise and respect the existence of legal pluralism is to acknowledge and celebrate the value of non-state law so as to promote both legitimacy and self-determination. With this explicitly in mind, we advanced criteria for legal pluralism designed to emphasise what we take to be the most morally pressing elements of this phenomenon. These were: first, that there must be a provisionally identifiable community of people governed by two or more seemingly distinct sets of governance practices. Second, that each such set of practices must ground at least some jural instances, which are *prima facie* morally binding for reasons of legality. Third, that there must be a belief on the part of at least some relevant individuals that these sets of governance practices are mutually incompatible. Fourth, that there must be no institution – that is, no court, legislature, council, or similar – with both the capacity and political legitimacy to authoritatively pronounce upon these apparent conflict(s). Our first two conditions serve to establish the possibility of legal pluralism within a given social space, whereas the second two operate so as to confirm its existence.

While advancing this account of plural legality, we identified a discrete philosophical problem that arises when the Rule of Law is viewed as a distinctive set of moral and political values. Insofar as legality concerns the importance of having an entire people subject to just one set of overarching governance principles, the existence of two or more such sets within a single social space would appear antithetical to the very idea of law. But that is precisely what legal pluralism would seem to entail. In response to this 'problem of plural legality', we contended that embracing the paradox is in fact often required by the very same set of values that ground and explain the existence of law as such. On this

DOI: 10.4324/9781003532149-5

Conclusion 99

view, legal pluralism must be recognised and maintained to the extent that civic equality, individual autonomy, political legitimacy, and collective self-determination mandate that course of action. In bringing our overall argument to its conclusion, we want to pass comment on one (perhaps controversial) implication that may arise from taking this normatively engaged, 'non-positivist' approach and, in so doing, leave our readers with a final insight into the nature of both law and legal pluralism, which strikes us as both fruitful and intriguing.

Legally pluralist thought can, in large part, be understood as a reaction against the idea that law is 'one big thing'.[1] The 'recalcitrant social reality' to which John Griffiths points is the 'interlegal' reality of multiple and overlapping normative orders, many of which are grounded in practices and traditions outwith the authority and control of the state.[2] We have largely endorsed this view, arguing that within many states, there are non-state normative orders that merit the dignity and respect often associated with law. Nonetheless, some readers may have found it counterintuitive that our endorsement of law's concrete plurality proceeds from an essentially universalist understanding of law itself. Law, or so we claim, turns on the instantiation of legality (or the Rule of Law) by concrete governance practices. But, on this view, the existence of both law and legal pluralism must turn on the same set of values *everywhere*: the constitutive values of legality are, for us, simply part of the nature of law. How can it be that we endorse both concrete plurality and conceptual universality? Is our non-positivist account of legal pluralism, with its argumentative premise that the nature and existence of law turns on a particular set of universal values, not just legal *monism* by another name?[3]

In one sense, this is true. It necessarily follows from our view of law that legal pluralism pertains only where the universal values of legality are instantiated in more than one conflicting legal order within any given social space. For us, law is 'one big thing' insofar as the Rule of Law has some degree of determinate normative content, albeit at a reasonably abstract level, and should be understood, in light of that content,

---

1 We take this phrase from: Ronald Dworkin, *Justice for Hedgehogs* (Harvard UP 2011) 1.

2 John Griffiths, 'What is Legal Pluralism?' (1986) 24 Journal of Legal Pluralism and Unofficial Law 1. On 'interlegality', see Boaventura de Sousa Santos, 'Law: A Map of Misreading. Toward a Postmodern Conception of Law' (1987) 14(3) Journal of Law and Society 279–302.

3 Legal monism, at its most basic, is that idea that the almost self-evident plurality of legal orders existing within our social world is an illusion: that every apparently separate order is in fact part of one overarching system. It stands, for example, in favour of the proposition that 'from the perspective of international law, all laws form part of the law of the world community' (Paul Gragl, *Legal Monism: Law, Philosophy, and Politics* (OUP 2018) 3).

as a discrete mode of association which separate peoples may institute in a plurality of different ways. But this is not monism of the same sort as that considered so illusory, fanciful, and dangerous by Griffiths and other early legal pluralists. The monism of state law is, as we emphasised in Chapter 1, one of centralism. State law claims absolute practical authority, and in both settler and postcolonial contexts, it does so often without regard for the importance of cultural, political, social, and spiritual identities not bound up with the larger political community that contemporary states represent. This sort of monism is what Nietzsche had in mind when referring to the state as 'the coldest of all cold monsters', within which 'all lose themselves, the good and the bad'.[4] It is a monism that tempts hegemony, domination, and normative imperialism. We are fundamentally opposed to monism of this kind: indeed, we argue that the value of law itself runs contrary to it in many cases. States can be worthy of respect to the extent that they constitute valuable political communities,[5] however this cannot justify their attempts to unsee, absorb, or destroy the many non-state legal orders that operate within their territories as crucial means for the self-determination of peoples at a substate level. Far from supporting this kind of thing, our views about the universal value of law supply weighty reasons why we cannot endorse such hegemonic practices.

The legal monism we espouse, to the extent that it deserves such a moniker at all, operates purely at the level of normative value. It holds law 'not [to be] a rival system of rules that might conflict with morality but as itself a branch of morality'.[6] To quote Dworkin, from whom we take this overall approach, 'morality in general . . . [has] a tree structure: law is a branch of political morality, which is itself a branch of a more general personal morality'.[7] Under the shade of this distinctive 'branch', individual legal orders necessarily exist in plurality because the governance practices that instantiate the values of legality are practised by real people in a messy and contested social world. And just as the moral principles that enjoin us to keep our promises can sometimes conflict with other principles that nonetheless all belong to the same tree-like structure, so too can law conflict, for example, with fairness, justice, or compassion. Moreover, since the values of law never appear in the world *in propria persona* but only insofar as they are instantiated within particular governance traditions, the form that instantiation

---

4 Friedrick Nietzsche, *Thus Spoke Zarathustra: A Book for Everyone and Nobody* (Graham Parks tr, OUP 2005) part I, ch XI 'The New Idol'.
5 See generally: Alex Green, *Statehood as Political Community: International Law and the Emergence of New States* (CUP 2024).
6 Dworkin (n 1) 5.
7 ibid.

takes will (as we have seen) vary considerably. In light of this, apparent and actual conflicts between different legal orders are almost inevitable. To continue the analogy, just as we might make individual promises that conflict notwithstanding the fact that each such promise binds us for the same set of genuine normative reasons, so too can different legal orders give rise to conflicting jural instances, notwithstanding the fact that their legal character is ultimately grounded upon the same set of values.

In this respect, ours is an inclusive and nuanced *philosophical* monism, which recognises a plurality of legal orders at the same time as ascribing unity to law as a discrete domain (or 'branch') of moral activity. It recognises the importance of non-hegemonic institutions and individuals having decision-making power in relation to the legal orders that govern them, particularly where the available hegemonic alternatives are beset by histories of colonial injustice. Law as such might be a matter of genuine practical reason, such that the true construction of legality's constitutive values does not turn on what any particular group of people say or believe. Nonetheless, the content of those values mandates that when it comes to their recognition and application, some voices – typically those of marginalised and oppressed peoples – matter more than others. This brings us to the intriguing point foreshadowed earlier. It seems possible that, for those that find our overall view persuasive, the commonplace conceptual juxtaposition of monism and pluralism (as opposed to state centralism and legal plurality, viewed as contrasting normative projects) may come to be seen as resting upon a false dichotomy. To see why, it pays briefly to examine two alternative positions.

Hans Kelsen famously argued for a particularly austere form of legal monism. Kelsen viewed law as monistic because he took the *presupposition* that all laws form part of the same system to be necessary for holding that conflicts between national and international law are logically impossible.[8] The absence of normative conflict matters, according to Kelsen, because acknowledging the existence of such conflicts would prevent us from adopting a coherent perspective from which *both* national and international law could count as systems of norms that make valid claims upon our behaviour.[9] Since, in Kelsen's view, adopting this perspective is essential for viewing both national and international law *as legal orders*, the two must, in fact, be part of the same normative system.[10] Leaving aside some of the logical difficulties with Kelsen's

---

8 Hans Kelsen, *General Theory of Law and State* (Anders Wedberg tr, Harvard UP 1945) 373.

9 ibid 363, 407–8.

10 ibid 410; Hans Kelsen, *Pure Theory of Law* (Max Knight tr, University of California Press 1967) 328–29.

102   Conclusion

argument,[11] its overarching problem would appear to be a lack of motivation. Why does it matter that we adopt a perspective along the lines that Kelsen suggests? The only conceivable answer would seem to be that there are genuine practical reasons for doing so, either because the norms of national and international law are at least *prima facie* binding or because both legal orders otherwise merit some degree of respect. But if we are correct in our view that both the provisional authority of law and the degree of respect that discrete legal orders deserve turns on an account of their value that itself mandates recognition of legal pluralism, then these additional normative premises cannot support monism, and Kelsen's argument remains unmotivated.

Now, consider views that occupy quite the opposite end of the spectrum, many of which were detailed in Chapter 1, including what Griffiths characterises as 'strong' legal pluralism,[12] what Merry names 'new legal pluralism',[13] and what Tamanaha calls 'folk law'.[14] It is once again worth quoting from Merry herself, who goes right to the heart of the issue currently at stake by posing what we in Chapter 1 called 'The Law Question':

> Where do we stop speaking of law and find ourselves simply describing social life? Is it useful to call all these forms of ordering law? In writing about legal pluralism, I find that once legal centralism has been vanquished, calling all forms of ordering that are not state law by the term law confounds the analysis.[15]

Underlying Merry's self-professed confoundment in this passage is, we believe, a justifiable concern about argumentative motivation, not unlike the one that plagues Kelsen. Early legal pluralists writing within both legal anthropology and legal sociology struggled to square their wholly justified concern that non-state law is often treated as possessing a 'lower conceptual status'[16] with their willingness to throw the doors as wide open as possible. Since, unlike us, they were unwilling to ascribe a central meaning to the idea of law that linked it in some meaningful way to claims about objective moral value, they necessarily lacked any

---

11 See generally: HLA Hart, 'Kelsen's Doctrine of the Unity of Law' in Stanley Paulson (ed), *Normativity and Norms: Critical Perspectives on Kelsenian Themes* (OUP 1999).

12 Anne Griffiths, 'Legal Pluralism' in Reza Banakar and Max Travers (eds), *An Introduction to Law and Social Theory* (Hart 2002) 302.

13 Sally Merry, 'Legal Pluralism' (1988) 22(5) Law and Society Review 869, 886–89.

14 Brian Tamanaha, 'Scientific versus Folk Legal Pluralism' (2021) 53(3) The Journal of Legal Pluralism and Unofficial Law 427, 435.

15 Merry (n 13) 878.

16 Franz von Benda-Beckmann, 'Legal Pluralism and Social Justice in Economic and Political Development' (2001) 32(1) IDS Bulletin 46, 48.

justifiable point at which to draw the line between law and not-law. However, by the very same token, they also lacked a fully articulated set of reasons for *extending* the category 'legal order' beyond those hegemonic normative orders attached to the state. For us, it is genuine normative reasons that do this work. Without them, it is difficult to see how any kind of definitional or taxonomical move could proceed with sufficient motivation. If the distinction between law and non-law is to matter at all, then it must matter *for moral reasons*. As such, an appeal to some kind of universal theory of legality, which takes a justifiable position on its value (however controversial that position might be), seems unavoidable. Insofar as it necessarily implies that law (capital 'L', as it were) is 'one big thing', this view might seem monistic. But since monism of this sort admits the very non-state orders that the anthropologist and sociologists wanted to admit, while guarding against the over inclusivity that gave them such pause, it surely cannot give us any cause for concern.

Index

American legitimacy crisis 67–76
Arendt, Hannah 43
Australia 7, 15–17, 32, 65, 76,
  79–81, 91
autonomy, individual 45–7

Barber, Nick 49
Burundi 83–4

Cameroon 92
Chatterjee, Partha 82
Chiba, Masaji 29, 31
civic equality 44–5
colonial injustice 60–65, 96–7;
  complicity of international
  law 89–96; customary law
  and land conflicts 83–9; *Mark
  Oliphant v. Suquamish Indian
  Tribe* 67–76; Mato Tipila and
  Uluṟu 76–81; postcolonial
  legal pluralism 82–96; and
  settler-states 65–7
common ground 83–9
complicity of international law
  89–96
conceptual development of legal
  pluralism 11–12; critical legal
  pluralism 32–4; interlegality
  24–8; 'The Law Question'
  17–19; 'messy compromise'
  12–17; non-Western and
  Global South perspectives
  28–32; social fact legal
  pluralism 20–4
conflicts, land 83–9

constitutive values 38–42, 44,
  53–5, 99–101
critical legal pluralism 32–4
customary law 83–9

Davies, Margaret 14–19, 26,
  32–4
Duthu, N Bruce 31
Dworkin, Ronald 40–2, 45, 73,
  100

equality, civic 44–5
existence of law 38–42

Fawole, W Alade 82
Finnis, John 41
Frankenberg, Günter 31
Fuller, Lon 36, 43–6

Gebeye, Berihun 83
Glenn, Patrick 28
Global South perspectives
  28–32
Green, Alex 62, 91
Griffiths, John 13–16, 22–3, 30,
  99, 100

Habermas, Jürgen 41
Hart, HLA 14, 20–4, 30,
  42–3, 67
Hobbes, Thomas 8

identification of law 40–2
illegitimacy 60–5
individual autonomy 45–7

Index

injustice 60–65, 96–7; complicity of international law 89–96; customary law and land conflicts 83–9; *Mark Oliphant v. Suquamish Indian Tribe* 67–76; Mato Tipila and Uluru 76–81; postcolonial legal pluralism 82–96; and settler-states 65–7
interlegality 24–8
international law 89–96

Jobani, Yuval 76

Kelsen, Hans 14, 93, 101–2

land conflicts 83–9
law, customary 83–9
law, existence of 38–42
law, identification of 40–2
law, international 89–96
law, value(s) of 35–7, 58–9; conditions for legal pluralism 53–4; constitutive values and existence of law 37–42; problem of plural legality 49–52; requirements for legality 42–9; self-determination 54–8
'Law Question, The' 3, 12, 17–19, 22–4, 102
learning 6–10
legality: plural 49–52; what legality requires 42–9
legal monism 99–101
legal pluralism 1–3; and colonial injustice 60–97; conceptual development of 11–34; conditions for 53–4; postcolonial 82–96; and self-determination 54–8; teaching and learning about 6–10
legitimacy, political 47–9
legitimacy crisis 67–76
Letsas, George 50–4

MacDonald, Roderick A 28
Manderson, Desmond 30

Mark Oliphant v. Suquamish Indian Tribe 67–76
Mato Tipila 76–81
Maxfield, Peter 74
Melissaris, Emmanuel 24, 27
Merry, Sally Engle 15–18, 24, 27, 83, 102
'messy compromise' 12–17
moral profiles 41, 61, 64

natural law 1, 20
Nietzche, Friedrick 100
non-law 22–3, 103
non-positivism 50
non-state law 3, 8, 15, 50–2, 83–4, 88, 96–8
non-Western perspectives 28–32
normative pluralism 3, 12, 22–3

Palmer, Michael 11
Perez, Nahshon 76
plurality 35–7, 58–9, 98–103; conditions for legal pluralism 53–4; constitutive values and existence of law 37–42; problem of plural legality 49–52; requirements for legality 42–9; and self-determination 54–8 *see also* legal pluralism
plural legality 2–4, 49–55, 59, 65, 98
point of departure 32–4
political legitimacy 47–9
political values 4, 35–6, 49, 98
postcolonial legal pluralism 82–3; and the complicity of international law 89–96; customary law and land conflicts 83–9
practical reasons 33, 39, 101–2
promissory reasons 39

Raz, Joseph 46
Rule of Law 35–7, 40–9, 52–4, 59, 98–9

106 Index

Santos, Boaventura de Sousa
25–7, 32
Schmid, Ulrike 86–8
self-determination 54–8
settler-states 65–7; *Mark
Oliphant v. Suquamish Indian
Tribe* 67–76; Mato Tipila and
Uluru 76–81
social fact legal pluralism
20–4
state law 13–18, 83–8, 100–102

Tamanaha, Brian Z 18–23, 84,
102
teaching 6–10
Tjamiwa, Tony 80
Twining, William 22–3, 25, 30,
38, 51

Uluru 76–81
United States 511, 65–8

universal plurality of law 98–103
unseen peoples 89–96

value(s) of law 35–7, 58–9;
conditions for legal pluralism
53–4; constitutive values
and existence of lwa 37–42;
problem of plural legality
49–52; requirements
for legality 42–9; self-
determination 54–8
Valverde, Mariana 26
von Benda-Beckmann, Franz
14, 21

Waldron, Jeremy 39–40, 46, 66
Watson, Irene 7, 31–2, 79, 91
Wind River Tribal Court 77

Zambia 84–8
Zhou, Ling 11